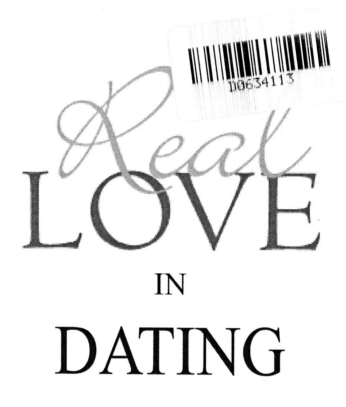

Real LOVE IN DATING

The Truth About Finding The Perfect Partner

GREG BAER, M.D.

Real Love in Dating — The Truth About Finding the Perfect Partner
Copyright © 2004 by Greg Baer, M.D.

Baer, M.D., Greg
     Real Love in Dating
     ISBN 1-892319-17-9
     1. Relationships 2. Self-help 3. Psychology
Second Edition
Published by:
Blue Ridge Press P.O. Box 3075 Rome, GA 30164
www.GregBaer.com

Also by Greg Baer, M.D.

Real Love — The Truth About Finding Unconditional Love and
    Fulfilling Relationships
      —Gotham Books
Real Love — The Truth About Finding Unconditional Love and
    Fulfilling Relationships, Unabridged Audio Book — Set of seven
    60 Minute CDs
      — Blue Ridge Press
The Real Love Companion
      — Blue Ridge Press
The Wise Man — The Truth About Sharing Real Love
      — Blue Ridge Press
Real Love in Marriage — The Truth About Finding Genuine
    Happiness in Marriage
      — Blue Ridge Press
Real Love in Parenting — The Truth about Raising Happy and
    Responsible Children
      — Blue Ridge Press
The Truth About Love and Lies — Set of three 60 minute CDs
      — Blue Ridge Press
The Healing Power of Real Love — set of two DVDs, total running
    time 2 Hours, 20 Minutes
      — Blue Ridge Press

Printed in the United States

Acknowledgments

I can't imagine writing a book alone. I have benefitted in so many ways from the support, advice, and experiences of others. At the risk of omitting many who have helped in the process of writing this particular book, I'd still like to make a stab at thanking a few. I especially appreciate:

My wife, Donna, without whom this work would be quite impossible.

Aurael Christall, Jeff Harness, Becky Witt, Cheryl Silva, Lynne Murray, Trudy Strombom, Susan Hadley, Jini Wimmer, Rosemary Radford, David Colella, and Mike Baer, for their helpful suggestions about content and grammar.

Tammy Jo Cook, for inspiration and proofreading.

Steve Smith, Leslie Tumlin, David Raucher, Patrick O'Leary, and Cameron Sharpe at SoulMate for their pioneering efforts in online dating.

The thousands of singles who have allowed me to learn as I've discussed the principles of Real Love with them.

REAL LOVE in DATING

The Truth About Finding the Perfect Partner

Chapter 1 GETTING THE FOUNDATION   1
RIGHT: What We All Really Want From
a Relationship

The Missing Ingredient—Real Love—
The Crippling Effect of Conditional
Love

Chapter 2 THE SECRETS OF FALLING IN   9
LOVE: The Real Reasons We Do, and
Why It Doesn't Last

Praise—Power—Pleasure—Safety—
Falling in Love—the Nature and Effect
of Imitation Love—The Real Reason
Relationships Fail—"I Love You
Because . . ."—The Repeating Pattern—
Freedom

Chapter 3 THE KISS OF DEATH: The Eight   27
Things You Don't Realize You're Doing
That Guarantee Disastrous Dates and
Lousy Relationships

Lying as a Getting Behavior and Lying
as a Protecting Behavior—Attacking
as a Getting Behavior and Attacking
as a Protecting Behavior—Acting like
Victims as a Getting Behavior and
Acting like Victims as a Protecting
Behavior—Clinging as a Getting
Behavior—Running as a Protecting
Behavior—The Tragic Effect of All

Getting and Protecting Behaviors—
Eliminating, Not Just Managing, Anger
from Our Lives

Chapter 4   MAKING THE BOLD MOVE: How   51
to Have Great Dates and Fulfilling
Relationships Every Time

Men and Women—Finding Real Love—
The Role of Faith in Telling the Truth
and Finding Real Love—Tell the Truth
to Whom—How to Tell the Truth—The
Effect of Feeling Real Love—The
Purpose of Dating—What If Your Date
Doesn't like the Truth about You?—Two
Keys to Great Relationships—Getting to
"No" Faster, or the Joy of Rejection—
The Truth about Relationships—The
Law of Expectations

Chapter 5   SPOTTING THE GOLD AND   101
AVOIDING THE ROCKS: What to
Look For—And What to Avoid—In a
Partner

The Criteria for Selecting a Partner—
How to Look for the Gold—Criteria to
Avoid: What Not to Look for—What to
Ask, and How to Evaluate it

Chapter 6   BUMPING UP THE YIELD: The   119
Techniques of Dating

When to Date—How Can You Meet
Men? How Can You Meet Women?—
Asking—What to Do on a First or
Second Date—What to Talk about—The
Details of Dating—Who to Date—

—End of the Date—Second Dates and
Beyond: No More Wondering

Chapter 7 THE MINE FIELD: Sex in Dating 153

Sex as a Form of Imitation Love—Sex as
a Distraction from Real Love—Infidelity

Chapter 8 THE "M" WORD: 173
Making the Commitment to Marriage

When Are You Ready to Marry?—Why
Do People Avoid Commitment?—How
Do You Handle a Partner Who Won't
Commit?—How Can You Know You've
Found the Perfect Man/woman?—The
Expectations of Marriage: Natural but
Deadly—The Real Purpose of Marriage

Chapter 9 DO I LEAVE, OR DO I STAY?:
What to Do with Difficult Relationships

Decide *Whether* Each Relationship
Can Be What You Want, Rather than
Trying to Make it What You Want—
End Relationships Sooner—End
Relationships Lovingly—After the
Break-up

Chapter One

Getting the
Foundation Right

What We All Really Want from a Relationship

If you're looking for a book that will give you a quick fix, or an easy technique that will magically produce personal happiness and great relationships, you're in the wrong place. In *Real Love in Dating*, you will learn the essential principles with which you can build a foundation for richly rewarding, long lasting relationships. This may require a change in how you see the people around you. It may require a change in who you are. In the process, however, you will become prepared to participate in the kind of loving, supportive relationships you've always wanted.

For years, Mark and Sharon dreamed of building a new home. They spent months finding the right piece of land, poring over architectural plans, and selecting doors, windows, carpets, and drapes. They were involved with every step of the construction—framing, bricklaying, sheetrocking—and when they finally moved in, they were excited beyond words.

For the first year in their new home, they could scarcely believe their good fortune, but shortly into the second year they noticed that some of the doors no longer shut properly. They took the doors off their hinges, shaved off some wood here and there, and the problem was solved. But then some of the windows wouldn't open, and small cracks began to appear in the walls. Repairs were made, but the problems returned, and finally the crack in the foundation became obvious. Eventually, the water and sewer lines broke, causing extensive damage in the house.

Mark and Sharon brought in a consultant, who discovered that the house rested on land that was once the bottom of a shallow lake. The soil was quite unstable, and the foundation had not been made sufficiently strong to withstand the shifting forces of the ground.

At that point, Mark and Susan could have poured great additional sums of money into repairing the windows and doors, but without addressing the critical problem of the faulty foundation, their problems would have continued. Despite their very best efforts to build the home of their dreams, they were obliged to tear it down.

THE MISSING INGREDIENT

Everywhere we look, we see relationships following a pattern similar to that which Mark and Sharon experienced with their home. Millions of us are out there looking for the "right person"—in bars, at parties, in clubs, at church, and on Internet dating sites—just as Mark and Sharon looked for all the right materials for their home. When we succeed in finding the person we're looking for, we fall in love, and often we get married.

But what happens after that? Almost 60% of marriages end in divorce, and 50% of married women have indicated that if not for finances and children, they would leave their husbands.

That leaves only 20% of marriages that would even *survive* if the partners felt they had a reasonable choice to leave. Of the marriages that remain, only a small number are genuinely happy. It is generous to say that 1-2% of all couples who marry end up with relationships that are as rewarding as they had once hoped.

If you knew that the odds of reaching your destination in a long journey, or of achieving success in a business, were between 50:1 and 100:1, would you start the journey, or invest all you had in the business? Of course not, and yet we don't hesitate to dive into dating and relationships with exactly those odds against us. And keep in mind that these terrible odds apply to relationships that made it all the way to marriage, where both partners were certain they had found exactly the right person.

> Do you really want to look for a serious relationship when the odds against finding genuine happiness are between 50:1 and 100:1? We need to learn more about relationships before we look for a partner.

It's clear that we need much more than additional ways to get together with potential partners. We already know how to do that. We don't need, for example, another Internet dating site that uses the meat market approach to selecting a partner. Matching people with psychological profiles isn't the answer, either. Finding a partner—even the right one—and falling in love just isn't enough. In almost every unhappy marriage, the two partners started off in love—that's why they got married in the first place. The problem is that most of us fall in love with the doors, windows, carpets, and drapes of a relationship. We are so excited about the beauty of the decorations that we don't see the flaws in the foundation. Without the right foundation, our relationships will fail, no matter what we do to enhance the beauty of the trimmings.

REAL LOVE

We all want richly rewarding relationships, but we often fail to realize that a healthy *relationship* is the natural result of two healthy *individuals*. A great relationship is much like a beautiful duet, played by two instruments. Before we can meaningfully participate in a duet, however, we must learn how to play an instrument by ourselves. Few of us are prepared to *be* the kind of happy and loving partner that a loving relationship requires.

The foundation of a relationship is a natural result of the ingredients provided by both partners, and that brings us to the central question: What do we all require before we can be happy as individuals? What quality must we possess individually before we can participate in a great relationship?

> A great relationship is much like a beautiful duet, played by two instruments. Before we can meaningfully participate in a duet, however, we must learn how to play an instrument by ourselves.

After World War I, there were a great number of orphans in Europe. At one large orphanage in Germany, a study revealed that nearly *three-fourths* of their infants under one year of age died despite the best hygiene, nutrition, medical care, and shelter. At about the same time, there were orphanages in the United States reporting death rates as high as *90%* for their infants, who had also received good nutrition and medical care.

Over a period of many years, civil authorities began to abandon orphanages in favor of placement in foster homes, and with that new practice, the horrific death rate of infants disappeared. In foster homes, the children were fed no better, nor were they kept any cleaner than in the institutions, but they were physically *handled* a great deal more than they ever were in the orphanages. The institutional orphans had become physically sick, and had died, simply because they were not shown physical affection. When they cried, they were not stroked and petted as infants in most homes usually are. It had not occurred to the administrators of those institutions that the babies needed to be held as much as they needed to be fed and washed. They literally *died* from a lack of love.

To this day, we all have the same urgent need for affection that those orphans did. We need love as much as we need food, water, and air, and without it we cannot be happy, nor can we have healthy relationships.

Not just any kind of love will do, however. The foundation of every healthy relationship—the one ingredient most essential to genuine happiness—is *Real Love*, unconditional love. When we have a sufficient supply of Real Love, our individual happiness is assured, and we have the ability to participate in vibrant, loving, and exciting relationships. Without Real Love, we can only struggle desperately to find a happiness that will never come, and we will experience only disappointment and frustration in our relationships.

> The foundation of all genuine happiness—and all rewarding relationships—is Real Love. With Real Love, nothing else matters; without it, nothing else is enough.

It's Real Love when I care about your happiness without any thought for what you might give me in return, and when you care about my happiness without any expectation of return for yourself. It's Real Love not when I do what you want and you like me—frankly, that's worthless. It's Real Love only when I'm flawed and foolish—when I get in your way and don't do as you wish—but you don't feel disappointed or irritated at me.

When someone is genuinely concerned about our happiness, we feel a profound connection to that person. We feel included in his or her life, and in that instant we are *no longer alone*, the condition most painful to us. Each moment of unconditional acceptance creates a living thread to the person who accepts us, and these threads weave a powerful bond that fills us with a genuine and lasting happiness. Nothing but Real Love can do that. In addition, when we know that even one person loves us unconditionally, we feel a connection to everyone else. We feel included in the family of all mankind, of which that one person is a part.

Regrettably, few of us have experienced much Real Love. Consider the experiences that almost all of us had as children. When we were quiet, clean, obedient, and cooperative, our parents, teachers, and others smiled at us. They spoke kind words and patted us tenderly on the head. We loved that, and we were willing to do almost anything to get those signs of acceptance and affection.

We also saw, however, that whenever we were loud, messy, and uncooperative, the smiles instantly disappeared. The tone of voice, and the choice of words, changed dramatically. Although it was unintentional, from these behaviors we heard this powerful message: When you're good, I love you, but when you're bad, I love you less—or not at all. There was no other way we could have interpreted how differently people treated us when we misbehaved.

Giving or withholding acceptance based on another person's behavior is the essence of conditional love, and nearly all of us were loved that way as children. Although it is given unintentionally, conditional acceptance has an unspeakably disastrous effect, because it fails to form the bonds of human connection created by Real Love. As a result, no matter how much conditional love we receive, we still feel empty, alone, and miserable, and without the foundation of Real Love, we cannot have healthy relationships.

Most of us spend a lifetime fussing with the doors and windows of life, completely unaware that our foundation is fatally flawed. If you've had difficulty finding and sustaining great relationships, it will not help you to focus on changing the individual characteristics—appearance, interests, habits—of your partner. If you're unhappy, your partner is not the cause. You're unhappy because you don't feel unconditionally loved yourself and because you're not sufficiently unconditionally loving toward others. Both conditions have existed for a long time, usually from early childhood. You need to learn how to build a foundation of Real Love, after which all the other pieces fall together with relative ease.

> If you're unhappy, your partner is not the cause. You're unhappy because you don't feel unconditionally loved yourself and because you're not sufficiently unconditionally loving toward others—conditions that have existed for a long time.

To learn a great deal more about Real Love—what it is, why we didn't receive it, and how to get it—read *Real Love, The Truth About Finding Unconditional Love and Fulfilling Relationships* (Go to http://www.gregbaer.com/book/book.asp).

THE CRIPPLING EFFECT OF CONDITIONAL LOVE

Real Love is "I care how **you** feel." Conditional love is "I like how you make **me** feel." Conditional love is what people give to us when we do what they want, and it's the only kind of love most of us have ever known. People have liked us more when we made them feel good, or at least when we did nothing to inconvenience them. In other words, with our behavior we've had to *buy* conditional love from the people around us.

It's critical that we be able to distinguish between Real Love and conditional love. When we can't do that, we tend to settle for giving and receiving conditional love, which leaves us empty, unhappy, and frustrated. Fortunately, there are two reliable signs that love is not genuine: *disappointment* and *anger*. Every time we frown, sigh with disappointment, speak harshly, or in any way express our anger at other people, we're communicating that we're not getting what **we** want. At least in that moment, we are not caring for our partner's happiness—only for our own. Our partner then senses our selfishness and feels disconnected from us and alone, no matter what we say or do.

If you can't distinguish between Real and conditional love, it won't matter how much effort you put into dating. You will almost certainly follow the path that has been blazed by the great masses before you, the path of giving and receiving the conditional love that can lead only to misery in relationships.

> Real Love is distinguished from everything else by the absence of disappointment and anger.

ℰ Chapter Two ℭ

The Secrets
of Falling in Love

The Real Reasons We Do,
and Why It Doesn't Last

If we don't have enough Real Love in our lives, the resulting emptiness is unbearable. We then compulsively try to fill our emptiness with whatever feels good in the moment—money, anger, sex, alcohol, drugs, violence, and the conditional approval of others. All those substitutes for Real Love become forms of Imitation Love, and they all fall into one or more of four categories:

- Praise
- Power
- Pleasure
- Safety

Let's discuss how we use these forms of Imitation Love, and how they affect our individual happiness and our ability to participate in relationships.

PRAISE

In the absence of sufficient Real Love, praise feels pretty good. From the time we were small children, we all experienced the exhilaration of hearing, "Good boy," or "Good girl," or "Nice job" when we behaved in the ways other people liked, and most of us have devoted the remainder of our lives to duplicating that feeling.

The pursuit of praise is so widespread that it's accepted as normal, even desirable. We've all heard, for example, the expressions "Put your best foot forward" and "Always make a good first impression." Without realizing it, our parents, teachers, and others taught us how to earn praise, and we accepted their counsel.

Putting your best foot forward, however, has significant drawbacks. Imagine that you read an advertisement in the paper that states, "Best apples you've ever eaten." Rushing down to the store, you find on display the most beautiful apples you've ever seen. The store clerk offers you a slice of one of the apples, and you discover that they taste every bit as good as they look. You buy an entire bushel and load them in the car. At home, in the first couple of days you eat nearly a dozen of the apples, and pat yourself on the back that you saw that newspaper advertisement. You even tell your friends about your good fortune. On the third day, however, after eating through two layers of the apples, you discover that all the rest of the apples are soft and old, and many are rotten.

Rushing back to the store, you confront the clerk about the rotten apples, saying, "You promised that these would be the best apples I'd ever eaten."

"But the apples on top were the best you'd ever eaten," said the clerk. "Am I right?"

"Well, I guess they were," you say, "but that's not the point. You lied to me."

"I did not lie," said the clerk. "I gave you the best apples you'd ever eaten, just as I promised."

"What about the rotten apples?" you protest.

"I delivered exactly what I promised," said the clerk. "I didn't tell you about the rotten ones, because then I knew you wouldn't buy the whole bushel—and you didn't ask me about them, either. You were happy enough when you bought them. It's not my fault that you didn't look through the bushel to see if it was the same on the bottom as the top."

It's quite obvious that the clerk lied to you—he completely misrepresented his product—but he did nothing different from what most of us do on a first date. Two people on a first date are engaging in a best foot festival, with each party diligently presenting his or her best characteristics. On the surface, that might appear commendable, but look at what happens after these two people put the best apples on top, and succeed in winning the praise, acceptance, and approval of the other. They both believe that the other person's best foot—his or her best apples—accurately represents who that person really is, and that's where the problems begin.

After two people successfully establish a relationship based on their best foot, they eventually discover that their partner is much more than a best foot—that, metaphorically, there is also the other foot, bad breath, and many other imperfections—and the resultant disappointment can be overwhelming. They feel deceived, cheated, betrayed, and understandably they vent their frustration on their partner. After all, they reason—silently and aloud—I used to be happy in my relationship with you, but now I'm not, so you must be withholding the happiness you once gave me.

When a relationship goes bad, our natural conclusion is that *our partner* has failed us in some way, breaking the unspoken contract we'd made together. But the real reason relationships fail is that from the beginning we established the relationship on something less than the complete truth. Expectations were created, and when those were not met—when the truth came out about who we were, and who our partners were—we felt as though our dreams had been crushed.

Relationships fail because we start them without the one ingredient—Real Love—most essential to happiness and fulfilling relationships. Without sufficient Real Love, neither partner has a foundation strong enough to create a healthy and mutually rewarding relationship. Without enough Real Love, the foundation of any relationship will be fatally flawed, and no amount of time, effort, and worry spent on the windows, doors, and carpets will ever create a healthy relationship. *With Real Love, nothing else matters; without it, nothing else is enough.*

> Most of us were taught to put our best foot forward, and to create a great first impression. Regrettably, our partners choose us on the basis of that falsely positive image, and when we can't maintain it, the results are enormous disappointment and bitterness.

Tragically, although Real Love is essential to happiness, most of us have never had consistent experiences with it, as discussed in Chapter One. Even though no amount of Imitation Love can ever fill our emptiness, it *does* feel good for a moment, and when we're in pain, we're only too eager to reach out for anything that makes us feel better, however superficial and fleeting that cure might be. To use a metaphor, what we'd really like is cookies that are warm and fresh out of the oven, with that unforgettable smell, taste, and texture. If we can't have freshly baked cookies, however, we'll take stale cookies over nothing at all.

Our obsession with praise as a form of Imitation Love can be illustrated by a study recently done at a major university. Of the incoming freshmen women that year, 65% were found to have a significant eating disorder—mostly bulimia and anorexia. These women were so eager to be praised for their appearance that they were willing to starve themselves or induce vomiting after meals. They were willing to physically injure themselves because all women know that physically beautiful women are treated quite differently from those who are not considered attractive. To demonstrate this, a group of social scientists studied the reactions of a large group of people to two women placed at opposite ends of the room—one woman a model, the other considerably less attractive by most standards. To the surprise of no one, the "unattractive" woman was treated virtually like a leper, while the model received a great deal of attention. This differential treatment was observed not only among the men at the gathering, but among the women as well.

Unintentionally, we teach our children from a young age—even in their bedtime stories—that it's very important to be praised for one's appearance. As a child, did you hear the fairy tale about the princess who was rather average looking? No, I didn't either. In our bedtime stories, we use the terms beautifulprincess and handsomeprince as though they were each one word. Without meaning to, we're teaching our children that they must be beautiful or handsome in order to earn the praise— and, by implication, the affection—of others.

As we vigorously engage in the pursuit of praise, however, we come to the terrible realization that the satisfaction it provides never lasts long. After you've worked for an hour, or a day, or a week, for example, to complete a project at work or elsewhere, it's quite satisfying to hear the approving words, "Nice job," but that feeling soon wears off, and then you have to work all over again to get another dose of it. The effects of praise are always short-lived, leaving us empty and desperate for more.

People who consistently use addictive drugs soon discover that the effect becomes increasingly brief, and more of the drug is required in order to achieve the same outcome. All the forms of Imitation Love are like an addictive drug. Despite all the effort required to earn Imitation Love, the beneficial effects of praise, power, money, and sex become increasingly brief. We also have to work harder to get the desired effect, and eventually we become exhausted and frustrated. Moreover, no matter how successful we are in obtaining Imitation Love, we never get the feeling of connection to other people that comes with Real Love, so we're still painfully alone.

A friend of mine used to interview celebrities on radio and television. She once interviewed a man who regularly performed on stage and screen. She asked him what it was like to be cheered and adored by so many, and he said, "It's a great feeling, but after the show, before I even get to the hotel in the limousine, I already need more." No amount of praise—or any other form of Imitation Love—is ever enough to make us happy.

> All the forms of Imitation Love become like an addictive drug: we must have more and more, and eventually no amount of it can give us relief from our pain.

Not only is the effect of praise brief, but somehow we also sense that it's not really about *us*. When people praise us, they're usually telling us that we've done something to make *them* feel better. When the boss praises you, is he saying that he's happy for *you*, happy that *you* have derived a sense of satisfaction and accomplishment from your performance? No, he's almost always saying that you've made *his* job easier, and he wants you to continue doing that.

When a man tells a woman that she is beautiful, to provide another example, is he really talking about *her*? Usually, what he's really saying is that he enjoys the physical pleasure of looking at her. He also enjoys the excitement of fantasizing about her, and if he persists in praising her beauty, he increases the chance that he might score an even greater physical pleasure with her. Without realizing it, when he says, "*You* are so beautiful," he's really saying, "I like how you make *me* feel."

POWER

When we don't have enough Real Love, we feel empty, alone, helpless, weak, and afraid. We get some measure of relief from those intolerable feelings, however, when we can control the behavior of other people. That sense of power feels much better than the helplessness we often endure. As we control people—as we convince them to agree with us, or to do what we want—we also get a sensation of connection to them, which relieves our loneliness.

In the absence of sufficient Real Love, power can be quite satisfying, and we get it in so many ways: with money, authority, physical and verbal intimidation, anger, violence, and sex. The following example will illustrate one common use of power.

In childhood, most young girls have little power over the people around them. They can't control their parents, teachers, friends, or even their own bedtimes. Without enough Real Love, this sense of helplessness is painful. When girls get older, however, and develop sexually, they can't help but discover that they have gained considerable influence over the boys and men around them. Sexually attractive girls tend to receive more attention, and they get away with more mistakes, than do girls who are less attractive. With their sexuality, young women learn to exercise power over others, and it's mostly unconscious. It's understandable that they would do that—we all naturally use whatever form of Imitation Love that will dull the pain of not feeling loved unconditionally.

PLEASURE

When we don't feel loved unconditionally, we use physical and emotional pleasures—sex, food, alcohol, drugs, shopping, gambling, driving fast, and so on—as welcome distractions, and we often pursue them with great devotion. The enjoyable effects of pleasure, however, are fleeting, and they can never make us genuinely happy in the absence of Real Love. If pleasure could produce the kind of happiness we all want, sex addicts would be the happiest people on the planet—but they're not. As with all the forms of Imitation Love, pleasure wears off, and eventually no amount of it will give us even a brief relief from our emptiness and pain.

SAFETY

Without Real Love, we're already in the worst kind of pain, and we'll go to great lengths to keep ourselves *safe* from experiencing more pain. If we can't have genuine acceptance, we can at least do everything in our power to avoid more disapproval. Toward that end, we avoid doing anything unfamiliar. We stay in the same boring, dead-end jobs, attempt to learn nothing new, and continue in stagnant, unrewarding—but predictable—relationships. If we've been hurt consistently by all our past relationships, but finally we're with someone who simply hurts us less, we can confuse that relative safety with love. Or we might avoid dating and relationships altogether.

FALLING IN LOVE—THE NATURE AND EFFECT OF IMITATION LOVE

Even though Imitation Love cannot give us genuine, lasting happiness, it *does feel good*, and if Real Love is either unknown to us, or unavailable, we'll go to great lengths to get enough Imitation Love to feel good temporarily. Stale cookies are better than nothing at all. In the absence of sufficient Real Love, we're strongly attracted to anyone who gives us Imitation Love, and it is therefore the pursuit of Imitation Love that governs how most relationships begin and end.

We've all observed that if we give enough praise, power, pleasure, and safety to someone, he or she will be more likely to return some of the same to us. In order to get the Imitation Love that can feel so good, therefore, we *buy* it with whatever forms of Imitation Love we have to offer. We trade Imitation Love with those around us. If I praise you enough, for example, you will be more likely to say something kind to me in return, or to do something else I want.

Without thinking about it, almost all of us tend to establish relationships based on the trading of Imitation Love. Let's arbitrarily measure Imitation Love in dollars, and we'll suppose that when you give a dollar of Imitation Love to someone, that person gives you twenty cents in return. To a second person you give a dollar, but in return you receive fifty cents. Without being aware of the reason, you naturally prefer the company of the person who gives you a fifty percent return on your investment— it's that better rate of return that determines why we "like" some people more than others.

Eventually, you give a dollar of Imitation Love to someone who gives you a full dollar in return. Excited about this dramatic improvement in your investment return, you give him or her two dollars, then three, then more, and to your delight, you are rewarded equally each time. This is so exciting that you are now "in love." Falling in love is rarely anything more than the relatively equal and abundant exchange of Imitation Love. That's not romantic, but it's nonetheless true. When a guy sees a girl across crowded room, and says to his friends, "I think I'm in love," is there anyone on the planet who believe that he's saying, "I've fallen into a sudden unconditional concern for her happiness"? No, we tend to start our relationships on the basis of how much Imitation Love we anticipate we'll receive from that partner, and that's a disastrous foundation for a relationship. We can see the effects of Imitation Love in the following account of the relationship between Michael and Susan.

> Falling in love is rarely anything more than the relatively equal and abundant exchange of Imitation Love—a formula for disaster.

Michael had said complimentary things to other people all his life, but when he gave them a dollar's worth of praise, he rarely got a dollar of praise, power, pleasure, and safety in return. Then he met Susan. When he gave her a dollar of praise—verbal and non-verbal—she immediately responded by accepting him (praise), doing some of the things he wanted (power), and physically touching him (pleasure)—at least a dollar's worth all together. So he gave her even more Imitation Love—the best he had to offer—and when she responded generously, he was so thrilled with the exchange that he called the feeling "falling in love."

Susan was attracted to Michael because he was good-looking, funny, smart, and kind to her, and because he had a good job—all of which gave her a sense of praise, pleasure, and safety. They fell in love because the exchange of Imitation Love was abundant and relatively equal.

Susan and Michael began their relationship because they found in their partner the qualities that would entertain them, make them feel worthwhile, and give them safety, not because they unconditionally loved one another. Most of us pick our partners for the same reasons—we look for someone who has qualities that will temporarily make *us* feel good, and in return we're quite willing to do the same for that person.

As I've said before, however, the effect of Imitation Love always fades, as Michael and Susan discovered. They really enjoyed the initial exchange of Imitation Love, but it wasn't long before that level of praise, power, and pleasure wasn't as rewarding as it once had been. When people say the "excitement has worn off" in a relationship, they're just describing the fleeting effects of Imitation Love. As we experience less "happiness" with Imitation Love, we naturally turn to the people closest to us to supply what we're missing, and understandably our partners feel resentful of our increased demands. Most of our relationships begin based on an unspoken understanding of how much Imitation Love our partners will give us, and how much we'll give them in return, and when we change the rules—when we give less or demand more—our partners don't like that.

As couples discover the transient effect of Imitation Love, they also invariably find that the exchange of Imitation Love becomes unfair. We can roughly quantify the trading—and fading—of Imitation Love over the course of Michael and Susan's relationship. In the beginning, they exchanged Imitation Love as summarized below:

Type of Imitation Love	Imitation Love (in dollars) Received in the Relationship by	
	Michael	Susan
Praise	5	5
Power	5	5
Pleasure	6	2
Safety	<u>1</u>	<u>5</u>
Total Imitation Love	17	17

In the beginning of their relationship, they both received five dollars of praise as each of them complimented the other for a variety of qualities, including sexual desirability. They were equally successful in getting the other to do the things they wanted (five dollars of power each). Michael got more physical pleasure from the relationship (mostly from sex) than Susan (six dollars versus two), but Susan got a greater sense of security (safety) from the relationship than Michael did (five dollars versus one). Because they experienced more Imitation Love from one another than with anyone else they had known, they were in love. After several months, however, the trading had changed:

Type of Imitation Love	Dollars Received in the Relationship by	
	Michael	Susan
Praise	1	1
Power	3	1
Pleasure	4	1
Safety	0	1
Total Imitation Love	8	4

They both discovered that the effect of flattery had quickly worn off, and that constantly earning it was exhausting, so neither of them was willing to continue their initial efforts to praise one another. Susan discovered she could hardly get Michael to do anything she wanted (one dollar of power vs. the five dollars she got in the beginning of their relationship), so she tended to reward him with nagging instead of praise. Without sufficient praise and appreciation, Michael had even less motivation to keep doing what Susan wanted. Susan, however, still did errands and other acts of kindness for Michael, so he got three dollars of power from getting her to do what he wanted (compared to the five dollars he once got). He still got four dollars of pleasure from the relationship (mostly from sex), while she got only one dollar (virtually nothing from sex but some from other forms of entertainment they enjoyed together). Susan's sense of safety had been reduced to a single dollar, because he often criticized her (attacking) and because she wasn't sure of his fidelity when he looked at other women. Michael felt no safety at all as Susan nagged him about everything.

What a miserable state of affairs. When they first met, what Michael and Susan both needed was Real Love, but neither of them had ever felt much unconditional love, so there was *no way* they could have loved one another as they needed. We simply can't give what we don't have. In the absence of Real Love, they offered one another what they did have—Imitation Love in its various forms—and they gave all they had. Imitation Love does feel good, and because they were both giving it with all their hearts, they were satisfied in the beginning of their relationship. When the effects wore off, however, and they each gave the other less of the various forms of Imitation Love, they felt like the rules of exchange had been violated. They were both faced with the horror that they were not going to get the happiness they'd hoped for all their lives.

> Relationships fail not because either partner did anything wrong, but because both of them came to the relationship without enough of the one thing—Real Love—essential to individual happiness and healthy relationships. They based their relationship on a counterfeit currency—Imitation Love—that cannot buy happiness.

Later in their relationship, Susan experienced more disappointment than Michael did. Not only was she disillusioned with the decline in her overall happiness (four dollars of Imitation Love versus seventeen in the beginning), but she sensed that their relationship was unfair (four dollars for her versus eight for Michael). It's common for one partner to believe the relationship is worse than the other partner does, because although both partners are far from genuinely happy, one of them—in this case, Michael—is getting more Imitation Love than the other. In addition, although Michael wasn't ecstatic about their relationship, he was relatively satisfied, because even though his total was down from seventeen dollars to eight, it was still better than what he enjoyed before finding Susan.

Sex as a form of Imitation Love deserves special attention, and I'll be addressing that subject in Chapter Seven.

THE REAL REASON RELATIONSHIPS FAIL

I have counseled with thousands of couples, most of them married. Remember that people usually get married only after they have sifted through many potential partners, finally choosing the one they believe will be the fulfillment of their dreams. Ideally, marriages should be the cream of all relationships, the best of the best.

And yet 60% of those dream relationships end in divorce, and the vast majority of those who remain married are settling for far less than they had once hoped for. When troubled couples come to me for counseling, invariably they ask some variation on the question, "What happened?" Both partners are absolutely befuddled, wondering how they went from being soulmates to combatants.

In their attempts to understand what happened, it's unavoidable that each partner would blame the other. After all, they reason, their partner once "made them happy," and now that happiness is gone. The inescapable conclusion is that their partner has somehow failed them, somehow withdrawn the joy they once magically dispensed at the beginning of the relationship.

After reading the first two chapters of this manual, however, you now understand the real reason relationships fail. When two people enter into a relationship without sufficient Real Love, their relationship is virtually doomed from the beginning. Both parties lack the one ingredient most essential to genuine happiness and fulfilling relationships, but in the beginning of their association they give one another enough Imitation Love that they achieve the *illusion* of happiness. It's better than anything they've had before, so it seems real. Then, when the effects of Imitation Love begin to wear off—as they always do—they're left with the horrifying realization that their dreams are so much dust.

Relationships fail not because of what each partner does or does not do. Relationships fail because they are not built on a foundation of Real Love, but instead are based on a counterfeit currency—Imitation Love—that can never buy happiness.

"I LOVE YOU BECAUSE . . ."

When someone says, "I love you because . . ." that person really has our attention. We're eager to hear what follows: " . . . because you're smart, beautiful, handsome, responsible, clever, witty, whatever." We absolutely adore hearing those flattering descriptions of ourselves. What we don't realize is that those seductive words also constitute the seeds of destruction in our relationships.

When someone tells you *why* he or she loves you, that person is describing the qualities you must have in order for him or her to *continue* loving you. You're now obligated to continue filling the expectations of that person.

When we don't have enough Real Love, we're eager to fill our emptiness with Imitation Love, and when we find someone who gives us an adequate supply, we're naturally drawn to that source. We must understand that when we say, "I love you," what we usually mean is, "I *need* you." When we don't feel unconditionally loved, and we tell someone we love him or her, we're expressing only a selfish wish for that person to keep making *us* feel good. When we say, "I love you," however, our partner hears us promise that we'll make *him* or *her* happy. These conflicting expectations cause the failure of most relationships.

When I discuss this subject in seminars, someone often asks, "So you're saying that if we had sufficient Real Love in our lives, we could love *everyone*?" When I reply in the affirmative, he or she continues, "But you're not saying that we should *date* or *marry* just anyone, are you? Isn't it all right that we look for certain qualities we like in a future spouse, for example? Isn't it all right to want to marry someone *because* they possess certain qualities I like? That's not necessarily selfish, is it?"

As we find sufficient Real Love in our lives—we'll discuss how to do that in Chapter Four—our emptiness and fear disappear. We're no longer driven by what we need from people, or by what we fear from them, and in that condition we then gain the ability to accept all people and care about their happiness.

Although we can certainly learn to accept and love everyone without their doing anything for us—the definition of Real Love—that doesn't mean we won't find some people more enjoyable to be around. We'll discuss that subject in greater detail in Chapter Five.

THE REPEATING PATTERN

Our pursuit of Imitation Love explains not only how relationships begin and end, but also explains how we tend to attract the same kind of partner over and over. How many times have you known someone who has broken up with a partner, and then, only a few weeks or months later, he or she has found the same partner but with a different face? Somehow we seem to find the same personality type over and over, as though we were magnets for that particular kind of person. Why do we keep repeating these same patterns of attraction and failure?

Without enough Real Love, we're desperately looking for those people who will give us a "good deal" in Imitation Love. It's as though we have a flashing billboard on our foreheads, which states, "Looking to trade." We advertise to potential partners that we're willing to give Imitation Love in exchange for receiving it. Over a lifetime, we have learned to offer a certain combination of the different forms of Imitation Love. We've all noticed, for example, that some of us are more likely to offer flattery to attract people, while others of us tend to offer power or pleasure. When we find someone who is attracted to our particular combination—say, for example, five parts praise, four parts power, two parts pleasure, and three parts safety—and when we in turn like the combination he or she offers us, everything "just clicks," and we're certain we've found the love of our life.

When everything "just clicks," however, it almost always means that we've just found a great exchange of Imitation Love, and that will never make us happy. The initial excitement, though, is enormously seductive, and we tend to fall for it over and over. Until we recognize what's happening, we're doomed to repeat this unhappy pattern.

> We keep repeating the same unproductive behaviors in relationships because we keep bringing the same person—ourselves—to each relationship. Until we learn to stop looking for Imitation Love, we will repeat our unhappy results over and over.

FREEDOM

As you come to understand Imitation Love, you may feel some sense of discouragement. You might think, "I can't believe it. I've wasted my whole life trying to find happiness with Imitation Love."

You're not alone. Most of us have unwittingly placed our faith in the utterly futile pursuit of the happiness that Imitation Love can never produce. Once we recognize this pattern, however, we can begin to take the steps that will lead to the Real Love, genuine happiness, and great relationships we've always wanted.

I once knew a woman who had a large house you simply would not believe. All the garbage she had generated over the years—old papers, empty food cans, rotten produce, car tires—had been tossed into the rooms that were not being used. Eventually the floors literally bowed with the weight of more garbage than I'd ever seen outside a regional landfill. Cockroaches were everywhere, and the only reason she wasn't overrun by rats was that she had thirty cats in the house. The cats generated their own waste, of course, and the combination of all that refuse created a stench that I would not have thought possible.

A group of friends decided to help this woman out of her predicament. With her permission, they arranged for the sale of the property on which the home sat—the home itself was bulldozed and burned—and helped her find a smaller, more manageable, apartment. They were so proud of themselves, that they had helped her find a more pleasant environment in which to live. Within a year, however, her small apartment looked almost exactly the same as her old home had. She had filled the place with garbage, and the stench of cat waste was overpowering.

Although these people had good intentions, they failed to consider that despite changing the woman's *location*, she herself had not changed, so the *cause* of the mess remained.

Most of us move from partner to partner, hoping that the next one will provide us the happiness we're looking for. If we bring to each relationship, however, the same inadequate tools—specifically a lack of Real Love—and a belief that Imitation love will bring us happiness, we will keep experiencing the same disappointing results, just as the woman who created a garbage dump wherever she went.

We must recognize our dependence on Imitation Love. Once we do that, we can begin to take the steps to find the Real Love we need.

To learn much more about Imitation Love—what it is, how it affects us, and how we can overcome our lust for it—read the book, *Real Love—The Truth About Finding Unconditional Love and Fulfilling Relationships* (Go to http://www.gregbaer.com/book/book.asp).

☙ *Chapter Three* ☜

The Kiss of Death

*The Eight Things You Don't Realize
You're Doing That Guarantee
Disastrous Dates and Lousy Relationships*

Without sufficient Real Love, we're consumed by two feelings: emptiness and fear. We feel empty because we don't have enough of the one ingredient most essential to genuine happiness, and in that condition we're also afraid that as we interact with other people, they will add to our pain.

In order to get the Imitation Love that will fill our emptiness, we use Getting Behaviors—lying, attacking, acting like victims, and clinging. To minimize our fear, we use Protecting Behaviors—lying, attacking, acting like victims, and running.

Let's discuss how we use these eight behaviors, and how they destroy any possibility of achieving the kind of dates and relationships we really want.

LYING AS A GETTING BEHAVIOR
AND
LYING AS A PROTECTING BEHAVIOR

To illustrate why we lie, let's observe an interaction between a four-year-old child, Andrew, and his mother, Suzanne.

Earlier in the day, Andrew had spilled red punch on the couch in the living room. An hour or so later, Suzanne stomped into the room where Andrew was playing, and in a harsh tone asked, "Who spilled something red all over my couch?"

When you're four years old, how big is your mother? She's King Kong, and when she's angry, that can be a fearsome sight, as it was for Andrew. On this particular occasion, Andrew unconsciously decided to follow the examples he'd seen of his older brother dealing with similar circumstances, and he responded, "I don't know."

Suzanne walked out of the room as she muttered something under her breath about how it *had* to be somebody. On this and other occasions, Andrew learned that when he lied, he tended to avoid getting into trouble. More accurately, Andrew lied to keep his mother from withdrawing her love, and that's the principal reason we continue to lie as adults. We hide the truth about our mistakes, flaws, fears, and foolishness because we've learned that people are then less likely to withdraw their approval—their "love"—from us.

How We Lie on Dates and in Relationships

Most of us lie a great deal more than we realize, and in light of the negative experiences we've had in the past when we let people see our flaws, our lies are quite understandable. In order to get people to like us, we project an image as positive as we can possibly create. We "put our best foot forward," as we discussed in Chapter Two. As we do so—using lying as a Getting Behavior—we're rewarded with Imitation Love in the forms of praise, power, and pleasure. We also lie to protect ourselves from the withdrawal of the approval we so badly desire.

Any time you do anything at all to earn the approval of another person—with how you look, what you say, what you do—you're lying. That sounds like a harsh thing to say, but think about it: when you look or behave a certain way in order to win the approval of someone, do you ever actually say to that person, "I'm doing this to impress you"? No, of course not, so you're not being honest. Yes, I know that almost *everyone* does this—they try to impress the people around them—but the fact that everyone is doing it doesn't make it honest or right.

> Any time you do anything to earn the approval of another person, you're lying, and that will have serious negative consequences in your relationships.

Following are some examples of how you might lie— usually unconsciously—to your date. In this chapter, as you read examples of each of the Getting and Protecting Behaviors, you'll notice that some of our behaviors fall into multiples categories. When we lie, for example, we might also be acting like victims and attacking someone at the same time.

- She asks you what kind of movies you like to watch, and you say, "*Sleepless in Seattle* and *You've Got Mail*," (a couple of real chick flicks for those of you who are clueless), even though you nearly threw up during those movies, and saw them only because dates from the past insisted that you see them.

- Politically, he's a passionate liberal/conservative, and you agree with the positions he describes, even though you really disagree with him, or you couldn't care less about the issues.

- He says, "The Super Bowl was unbelievable last night, wasn't it?" Even though you don't care the first thing about football, and know absolutely nothing about it, you did hear that the final score was 28-24, and you heard your brother talking about it. But you don't admit that you didn't see it. Instead you say, "Yes, it was a really close game, wasn't it?"

- You're late arriving at her house on a Saturday night, and you say, "Sorry I'm late. I was working out at the gym," even though the last time you visited the gym was two belt notches ago.

- He's wild about heavy metal music, and you don't tell him that the only music you listen to is classical.

- You tell her you're not married, when the truth is, you're only *separated* from your wife, not divorced.

- You pick a dress that gives him a cleavage demo, something you never do at work or home. You give the message that you're offering sex, even though you have no intention of having sex that night.

- You say you're 5'10". Sure, in three inch lifts—and if you count your hair.

- Through your words and behavior, you put out the message that you're a real fan of casual sex, while the truth is that when you have sex with a man, you have enormous romantic expectations.

- You invite her to a really fancy restaurant for a first date, much nicer than you would ever go to on your own. That may not seem like a lie, but it's not who you really are, is it?

- You say you're twenty- nine, which would be true only if you'd graduated from high school at age four.

- Your partner obviously drinks, so you have a drink with her—just to be sociable—even though you don't normally drink yourself.

- When your date asks if it's all right if he smokes, you say "Sure," even though you really don't like smoking.

- Your date asks if you like children—she has two at home—and you say you love them, even though you look at children as an infinitesimal step above rodents.

- He asks if you're involved with anyone. You respond, "Not really," even though the whole reason you're out on this date is to infuriate your boyfriend.

- You say, "I'm too tired to drive myself home, can I sleep on your couch tonight? I promise not to be a bother," when you're really hoping to score an intimate encounter.

- You say, "I had a great time," when you don't mean it.

- You say, "I'll call you," when you don't mean it.

- She asks if you like sushi, and you respond enthusiastically that you love to try new things, even though you haven't eaten anything but hamburgers and fries for the past decade.

- Your date expresses an opinion against drinking, so you refrain from drinking during the date, even though you would normally get as sloshed as possible.

- You say you quit smoking, even though you quit only five minutes ago.

- You smile excessively throughout the date, even though you can't wait for the experience to end.

- You go on a "quick diet" before the date.

- You let your answering machine pick up when you're home.

- You wear a push-up or padded bra, or control-top pantyhose.

- In the car with your date, you listen to music you think would impress him or her, instead of the trash you really like.

- You take relatively neutral positions on just about everything to avoid conflict and the possibility that he or she might not like you.

- You spend money much more lavishly with him or her than you normally would, hoping to create the appearance of success.

- You wear cologne or a necktie when you can't stand either.

- You insist on paying for your own dinner, with the explanation that you just like to share the expense, when the real reason is that you don't want to feel bad later if you ignore his calls.

- You say you'd "love to go" to the opera or some other cultural event, when you'd rather have your foot run over by a truck.

- You exaggerate your income or position at work.

- You name important people you know, and you exaggerate your connection to them.

- You ask frivolous or meaningless questions, not because you're really interested in the answers but because you're uncomfortable with those moments of silence that invariably occur on a date.

- You say I've "always wanted to do that" when your partner discusses her hobbies, when the truth is, you couldn't care less about clogging or making pottery.

- You post an old picture of yourself on a singles website to create the appearance that you're much younger than you are.

- You talk about how helpful you are to your elderly neighbour, when all you did was shovel his driveway once, two winters ago.

- You exaggerate the success in your career so she'll think you're an important man at work.

- You minimize your faults and maximize the faults of your ex-partners, blaming them for everything that was wrong with the relationship.

- You drive a new Beamer even though you can only afford a Ford.

- You say, "Most guys start pushing for sex by the second date, but I'm not like that." Then on the second date you invite her to your place, and you start pouring the daquiris.

Almost all these lies are told unconsciously. In the absence of sufficient Real Love, we simply cannot tolerate being without the Imitation Love that temporarily makes us feel better, and our lies help us to gain—and keep from losing—these substitutes for Real Love.

The Problem with Lying

So what is so terribly wrong with these unconscious lies we tell as we try to create a good impression and avoid the disapproval of others?

What we want most is to feel the unconditional love of others, to know that they care about our happiness regardless of our mistakes, flaws, and fears. Before you can feel my unconditional concern for your happiness (Real Love), however, you first must feel that I unconditionally accept you for who you really are. You can't feel loved until you first feel accepted, which we can illustrate with the following brief diagram:

Accepted → Loved

Similarly, you can't feel that I accept who you really are until you're certain that I actually *see* who you really are:

Seen → Accepted → Loved

And you can't be certain that I see who you really are until you tell me the *truth* about yourself:

Truth → Seen → Accepted → Loved

The process of feeling unconditionally loved can begin only when you tell the truth about yourself. The tragedy of lying, therefore, is that when we lie, we simply can't feel loved.

Dating highlights the problems of lying. Almost invariably, when we go out on a first date, we're working very hard to create a great impression. That might seem like a good thing to do, but what happens if we actually succeed? What happens when our partners indicate that they like what they see? Now we're trapped. Now we have to continue creating great impressions all the time, because we're afraid if our partners see who we really are, they won't like us. The effort of constantly projecting a positive image is exhausting.

Whenever you do anything at all to get someone to like you, it's as though you're putting up a false image of yourself—a cardboard cutout of you looking your best. And then *you* are not really there at all. You're not even present in the relationship. No matter what affection you earn from your partners, their relationship is with your image, not with you, and that deception can only lead to disaster down the road.

> We often hide our mistakes and flaws—we lie—because we don't want people to withdraw their approval from us, but the moment we lie, we make it impossible to feel loved.

In Chapter Four, we'll talk about how to break out of this pattern of lying, and how to establish relationships based on the truth and Real Love.

ATTACKING AS A GETTING BEHAVIOR
AND
ATTACKING AS A PROTECTING BEHAVIOR

Attacking is any behavior we use to motivate another person through *fear* to do what we want. The most common form of attacking is anger. When we're angry, we can often intimidate people to stop hurting us—which they're usually doing with *their* anger. With anger, we can also make most people sufficiently uncomfortable (afraid) that they'll do whatever we want in order to stop us from making them feel bad. With our anger, we can get people to give us attention, respect, power, flattery, approval, even sex.

How We Use Anger with Our Dates

In our society, anger—along with other forms of attacking—is so common that we scarcely notice it. Most of us become irritated many times a day—at other drivers on the road, at our bosses, at people who make us wait, and so on. We attack other people with guilt, physical intimidation, authority, criticism, and our attempts to control them.

We often attack the people we date, too, and we need to see how we do that. Following are just a few examples of attacking, which includes anger, guilt, and controlling:

- When you arrive to pick her up, she's not ready. With an impatient sigh, you roll your eyes and say, "We're going to be late." It seems like a small thing, but the impatience clearly communicates that she is defective, and that she has inconvenienced Your Royal Highness.

- You're headed out the door, and she says, "Are you going to wear *that?*"

- After the first date, you don't call for a week. When you finally do, she says, with an unmistakable tone of annoyance, "It's been a week."

- You resist his sexual advances, and he becomes irritated. The irritation is an attack, and a way of intimidating you to do what he wants.

- You get lost on the way to the restaurant, and she says, "You don't know where you're going, do you?"

- In the car, you describe a faster way to get where you're going, and with a scowl on his face he says, "I think I can handle this on my own. I've been driving without you for ten years now."

- You're listening to your favorite music, and she says, "You actually like that?"

- You're describing to someone else an event you saw on television, and your date jumps in and takes over the story you wanted to tell.

- She says, "You *forgot* it was Valentine's Day?"

- She asks you to do something you hate, and you respond testily with, "Are you kidding?!"

- She says, "Are you completely insensitive?"

- You ask your partner to do something, and even though it's obvious that he or she doesn't want to, you keep asking.

- Your date takes a long time deciding what to order for dinner, and finally you say, "Can't you just pick something?"

- You know you're late getting ready for a date, but you don't hurry one bit, dragging it out to make your date pay for some offense.

- You gossip about somebody you know, knowing it will hurt that person's reputation in the eyes of the person you're talking to.

- You roll your eyes when your date says he or she has to go back into the house to get yet another thing he or she has forgotten.

The Uniformly Negative Effects of Anger

We use anger to protect ourselves, and to get Imitation Love, only in an attempt to eliminate the emptiness and pain of not having enough Real Love. Anger temporarily makes us feel less helpless and empty. The use of anger, however, has terrible drawbacks. Can you think of a single time you got angry at someone and then felt *closer* to him or her? There's a reason for that. Every time you get angry at another person, he or she hears you say—with your words and your behavior—only four words: "I don't love you." If you have any doubt about that, blow up at someone today—anyone: boyfriend, girlfriend, child, parent, co-worker—and watch the expression on that person's face.

When I'm angry at you, I'm saying that you have failed to do something for *me*. You have dared to inconvenience what you may not have realized is the true center of the universe: *me*. We could accurately replace the word *angry* with *me-me-me*, and I promise you that other people feel that sentiment. Every time we get angry, we feel less happy ourselves, the people around us certainly hate it, and our relationships are seriously injured.

So Why Do We Get Angry?

If anger has such terrible effects, why do we continue to get angry? In great part, we're just reflexively mimicking what we've seen other people in our lives do—parents, teachers, and others—when *we* made mistakes. When we spilled the milk, fought with our sister, and dragged mud across the living room carpet, other people instantly became impatient and irritated. We saw them frown, roll their eyes, tap their feet, and glare at us. We heard their tone of voice change dramatically. Now, when other people make mistakes, we also get angry, simply following the innumerable examples we've seen as both children and adults.

There's a second reason we get angry at people who inconvenience us. In our society, it is almost universally accepted that anger is an unavoidable reaction to the negative experiences we encounter every day. Look at how often we think or say, "He (or she) makes me angry," or "You make me so mad." We honestly believe that other people make us angry. Regrettably, as long as we believe that, we're absolutely stuck with our anger. If I believe you "make" me angry, I become your puppet. At any time, you can choose to make me angry. You are in control of how I feel.

Fortunately, once we understand the roles of Real Love and anger, we can see that we always have a choice about how we feel. At the end of the chapter, we'll discuss how we can eliminate anger from our lives, and choose to feel loved, loving, and happy instead.

ACTING LIKE VICTIMS AS A GETTING BEHAVIOR AND
ACTING LIKE VICTIMS AS A PROTECTING BEHAVIOR

If we can convince people that we've been injured and treated unfairly, they'll often stop hurting us, and may even give us their sympathy, attention, and support. That's why we act like victims. Victims use variations on the following three themes: (1) Look what you did *to* me; (2) Look what you should have done *for* me; and (3) It's not my fault. Victims have excuses for everything and blame everyone but themselves for their own mistakes and unhappiness. We've all acted like victims at times. You're acting like a victim when:

- You're late, and you say "the traffic was bad." Sure, the traffic is sometimes bad, but if I promised you a million dollars to be ready on time for a date tomorrow, would you be there on time? Sure you would. We're late because we're insufficiently motivated to arrive on time, to plan ahead for contingencies that would make us late.

- A conversation gets difficult, and you break into tears.

- You didn't complete an assigned task, and you claim

you "didn't have time." Of course, you *did* have time to watch television, go shopping, and do everything else you wanted to do.

- Your partner does something you don't like, and you act hurt.

- You're offended when your partner forgets your birthday, Valentine's Day, and so on.

- You make a poor choice and claim, "I couldn't help it."

- You're offended when other people inconvenience you in any way.

- You say, "You just don't appreciate anything I do for you."

- You say, "After all I've done for *you*, you can't do this one thing for me?"

- You say, "Why can you never remember to put the toilet seat back down?"

- You're telling a story about getting a speeding ticket, and you make it the policeman's fault.

- Your boyfriend is glued to the football game on television, and you act hurt that he's not paying more attention to you.

- You sit and complain about conditions—the room being too cold, the music too loud, and so on—instead of living with it, taking action to change the circumstances, or leaving.

- You whine about how things are "unfair."

- You talk about all the terrible, hurtful things your ex-partners, family, and co-workers have done to you.

When we act like victims, we often succeed in protecting ourselves, and we often get the sympathy we're looking for, but no matter how much safety and sympathy we achieve, we can never feel loved unconditionally, because what we receive wasn't freely given. We had to manipulate people with our victimhood to get what we wanted. Victims don't feel loved. With their behavior, they succeed only in further isolating themselves from others.

CLINGING AS A GETTING BEHAVIOR

Without sufficient Real Love, we are desperate for any source of Imitation Love we can find. Once we find someone who will give us some of the time and attention we want, we tend to cling tightly to that person, sucking from them whatever acceptance we can get. You can cling in some of the following ways:

- You say, "Do you have to play golf this weekend?"

- You say, "We hardly ever spend any time together."

- He says he doesn't want to go out tonight, and you get that pained look on your face as you say, "Come on. Just for a little while?"

- You do something nice for her, and when she doesn't express any gratitude, you say, "Did you like the_____?"

- You cook a great dinner for him, hoping that as a result he'll agree to something you want him to do for you.

- He buys you a gift, and you thank him all over the place, unconsciously hoping that if you're sufficiently grateful, he'll be encouraged to do something like that again.

- "You're leaving me?"

- When he fails to call you later, as he said he'd do, you become upset.

- You're at a party with your date, and you become irritated when he doesn't spend as much time with you as you think he should.

- You're on the phone with your partner. When he or she says, "Well, I have to go," you keep the conversation going for another fifteen minutes.

- You fish for compliments. "Do you like my dress?" Or "How do I look?"

- Saying "I love you" for the purpose of getting an "I love you" in return.

- She has an early appointment on Saturday morning and ends the Friday evening date at 10:00. You say, "Do you have to go home so early?"

- You've had a really nice time at lunch. She says, "I'd like to spend the whole day together."

- He calls you 3 times a day to see how and what you're doing.

RUNNING AS A PROTECTING BEHAVIOR

One way to avoid pain is simply to run from it. You can do that in so many ways, on a date and otherwise:

- When you allow yourself the excuse of being "shy," which is really just a way of avoiding opportunities for other people to see you as you are.

- When a conversation becomes difficult, you stomp out of the room in a righteous huff. As you slam the door, you throw in a dash of attacking and acting like a victim as well—kind of a Protecting Behavior salad, as it were.

- By drinking in social situations, which enables you to escape from your fear and pain just enough to make interaction with others tolerable.

- By avoiding social situations—dating, parties, church, and other gatherings—so you don't have to face the pain of possible rejection.

- After you have a difficult interaction with your partner, you don't call him/her—or return calls—for several days.

- By keeping your answering machine on all the time, so you can screen your calls.

- By using drugs, which gives you a way to run from the emptiness and pain in your life.

- You hide who you really are from others, avoiding exposure to the possibility of being seen.

- You take relatively neutral positions on just about everything to avoid conflict and the possibility that your date might not like you.

- You're bored with the conversation, so you just drift off, taking a mental vacation.

- At a party, you spend as much time as possible with people other than your date.

- By claiming you "have a headache" in order to avoid interaction.

- When a third person calls you while you're on a date, you spend as much time as possible on the call, to avoid having to talk with your date.

- You sleep way too much.

- By taking a different route on foot or by car, to avoid someone you know you might otherwise encounter.

- By changing the subject when it becomes uncomfortable for you.

- You insist that your future plans are uncertain in order to avoid commitment: "For now, let's just keep going out and see where it goes, because I might get transferred."

- By saying you have a lot on your mind, thereby avoiding the responsibility of dealing with the present.

- You play computer games for hours on end.

- When your date asks if it's all right if he smokes, you say "Sure," even though you really don't like smoking." You're running from a potentially difficult conversation.

- By staying at work for longer than necessary, for the purpose of avoiding the emptiness in the rest of your life.

- You're always ready to end the relationship at a moment's notice if you don't get what you want.

- You've been dating this person for months, and the relationship is going well, but you keep a list of potential replacement partners waiting in the wings.

To be sure, all the forms of running do give us a brief relief from our pain, but they also have the uniform effect of making us feel alone, the worst condition of all, and the one we're trying to avoid.

THE TRAGIC EFFECT OF ALL GETTING AND PROTECTING BEHAVIORS

We use Getting Behaviors only because we feel empty and alone. We lie, attack, act like victims, and cling only in the hope that we might get the "love" we're sorely missing. Regrettably, the attention and "acceptance" we receive from Getting Behaviors can feel only like Imitation Love. Even on the occasions that people actually give us Real Love, when we're using Getting Behaviors we can *feel* only Imitation Love, because deep down we know we've purchased that attention with our manipulations. The more we use Getting Behaviors, the more empty and alone we feel. With all the Protecting Behaviors, we also feel more alone, because we're using them to keep people away from us.

It is perhaps the ultimate irony, then, that we use Getting and Protecting Behaviors to keep from feeling unloved and alone, and yet those behaviors cause the very conditions we are trying to avoid. We can never feel unconditionally loved as long as we participate in lying, attacking, acting like victims, clinging, and running. Regrettably, however, those are exactly the behaviors we learned as children, and so we instinctively continue to use them as adults whenever we feel empty and afraid.

When the effects of Imitation Love begin to wear off in a relationship, we immediately react—almost involuntarily, like a reflex—with the Getting and Protecting Behaviors. Every time you use those behaviors, however, your motivation is to get something for *yourself*, and to protect *yourself*. While you are fixated on your own selfish interests, is there any way your partner can feel your unconditional concern for his or her happiness? No, absolutely not, so here is the impossible situation you're in:

1. As your partner feels the effects of Imitation Love wear off in your relationship, he or she feels more empty and afraid.

2. To eliminate those dreadful feelings, he then uses Getting and Protecting Behaviors.

3. The instant he uses Getting and Protecting Behaviors, you feel his selfish motivation. You hear him say, "I don't care about you, only about myself—about my own needs and fears."

4. After hearing "I don't love you," you feel more empty and afraid yourself.

5. To eliminate those feelings in yourself, you respond with your own Getting and Protecting Behaviors.

6. Your partner accurately interprets your behavior as unloving, and then is even *more* likely to respond with additional Getting and Protecting Behaviors.

7. This self-perpetuating and self-destructive pattern escalates until you both become frantic, saying and doing things that can cause only enormous wounds in your relationship.

Until we can see that our own behaviors worsen the conditions we fear most, we are hopelessly trapped in situations and relationships that are endlessly painful. With greater understanding, however, we can begin to change our lives.

> We use Getting and Protecting Behaviors so that we won't feel unloved and alone. It is perhaps the ultimate irony that the instant we use those behaviors, we can't feel loved.

ELIMINATING ANGER FROM OUR LIVES—NOT JUST MANAGING IT

Once we understand the critical role of Real Love in our lives, and why we use Getting and Protecting Behaviors, we can begin to take huge strides in changing how we see other people, and how we behave toward them.

If Getting and Protecting Behaviors are responses only to our emptiness and fear, the solution to those behaviors is obvious. As we get more Real Love, our emptiness and fear disappear, and then our *need* for Getting and Protecting Behaviors simply evaporates. With Real love, we just lose our *reason* to lie, attack, act like victims, cling, and run. Real Love has the same effect on the Getting and Protecting Behaviors of other people. We'll discuss how to get Real Love—and the effect it has on us individually and in our relationships—in Chapter Four.

Even before we have sufficient Real Love in our lives, it is possible for us to greatly diminish our use of Getting and Protecting Behaviors. Let me illustrate the power we can gain over just one of those behaviors—anger.

Two Dollars Vs. Twenty Million Dollars

Earlier in this chapter I mentioned how we render ourselves puppets as soon as we believe that other people make us angry.

Imagine the freedom that would result if we all knew that other people *never* make us angry. If I become angry at you, for example, and I remember that your behavior cannot "make" me angry, how long could I continue being irritated at you? I'd look pretty silly to be angry at you when I knew you were not the cause. So let's prove the premise that other people don't make us angry.

Imagine that you're starving, and you're preparing to go out and get some bread with your last two dollars. This is an important moment. Suddenly, I dash into the room, snatch the two dollars off the table, and run away before you can stop me. Almost certainly you'd be angry at me, and very likely you'd say I *made* you angry. On the surface, the sequence of events and the logic do seem to support your claim:

- To start with, you were not angry.

- I came into the room and did something that affected you in a negative way.

- *Immediately*, you became angry.

- If I hadn't done what I did, it's likely you would not have become angry.

- The only reasonable conclusion is that I *caused* your anger, right?

No. The real cause of your anger is an underlying, pre-existing condition that we've failed to identify. Let's prove it.

Now imagine that the next day I do exactly the same thing—steal two dollars off the table as you're getting ready to go out and buy some bread—but this time you have twenty *million* dollars in the bank. What percent of twenty million is two? The loss of two dollars is insignificant in the presence of twenty million, so your reaction would be quite different from the first occasion. You might even stop me to offer me another two dollars.

It's now clear that my taking two dollars was not the cause of your anger in the first situation. If the act of taking two dollars had the power to *make* you angry, it would have made you angry on both occasions—but it didn't. You became angry on the first day because *you* didn't have twenty million dollars.

This is much more than a cute metaphor. In real life people do little things that inconvenience us every day—they're late, break promises, cut in front of us in traffic, and so on—each time taking two emotional dollars from us. If we're down to our *last* two dollars, each event becomes a pretty big deal. If, on the other hand, we have twenty million emotional dollars, such inconveniences become inconsequential. When we have sufficient Real Love—when we have the greatest treasure in life—we feel like we have twenty million dollars all the time. In that condition, when people are inconsiderate, when they fail to do what we want, and even when they attack us, they're taking only two dollars, which we can easily afford to lose. When we feel unconditionally loved, everything else becomes relatively insignificant.

We must understand, therefore, that how we react to other people is largely determined by how unconditionally loved we feel and not by their behavior. Without Real Love, we're starving to death and down to our last two dollars. In that condition, we're limited in our ability to remain happy and loving when a thief steals our money. Children who are raised without unconditional love can only be *severely* affected as they attempt to find happiness in the absence of the ingredient most essential for emotional and spiritual health. If that lack of Real Love is not corrected, a child will then become an adult who feels empty and afraid, and who will respond to others with Getting and Protecting Behaviors—which makes happiness and loving relationships impossible.

When we clearly understand that every time we're angry, *we* are the problem—that it is *we* who do not have the twenty million dollars we need—it is much more difficult to remain angry at anyone.

> Other people never *make* us angry. Rather, our anger is a reaction to a lifelong lack of Real Love in our own lives.

Drowning

To further help you let go of your anger at others, allow me to use another metaphor. Take your time reading this, and allow these principles to change the way you see the world.

Imagine that you and I are having a pleasant lunch together by the side of a large pool at a beautiful resort. The temperature is perfect, a light breeze is blowing, the palm trees are swaying, and in the distance you can hear a live band playing your favorite music. This is a *perfect* day. But then you notice that some man in the pool is splashing you with water—at first on your shoes, but then higher up on your ankles, legs, pants, skirt. You can't see who's splashing you because there's a deck chair between you and the person in the pool, but the water keeps coming at you from over and under the chair.

At first you ignore the splashing, but after a while you're really getting wet, and finally you become irritated and get up from your chair to say something to this idiot who's being so thoughtless. He has really spoiled your perfect day. As you stand up to look over the chair and say something to this careless buffoon, you see that the man splashing you is *drowning*. He's splashing you only because he's trying to keep his head above water.

Are you still mad at him? Of course not. How long did you have to struggle to lose your anger? The instant you saw what was happening, your anger was gone. How powerful it is to realize that a moment of understanding can completely change your feelings.

As you see the condition of the man in the pool, not only do you lose your anger, but you are immediately overwhelmed with a desire to help him out of the pool. What a miracle! In a single moment, you traveled the emotional spectrum from angry to not angry to unconditional concern for his well-being—the definition of Real Love.

You can achieve this kind of miraculous change in attitude in real life, too. Picture for a moment someone in your life who is irritating. Now picture their behaviors that annoy you. Can you see that every one of those behaviors is one or more of the Getting and Protecting Behaviors? Without exception, that is the case. And people use Getting and Protecting Behaviors for what reason? Because they're empty and afraid, a result of not having enough Real Love. Their need for Real Love is just as critical as the need of a drowning man for air.

All the people in your life who are behaving badly are just drowning, and they're using Getting and Protecting Behaviors only to keep their own heads above water. Their drowning doesn't have anything to do with you. It's not personal. Nobody drowns *to you.* As people do their very best to keep from drowning, however, it's inevitable that they splash the people around them, and the closer you are to them, the more you'll be affected.

When we can see angry people—or people using any of the Getting and Protecting Behaviors—as drowning, how can we possibly stay angry at them?

> When people behave badly, they're just drowning and using the Getting and Protecting Behaviors that temporarily keep their heads above water. When we understand and remember this, we lose our anger at the drowning people in our lives.

We talk more in subsequent chapters about how we can offer assistance—if we offer assistance at all—to people who are drowning.

To learn more about Getting and Protecting Behaviors—what they are, how they affect us, and how we can eliminate them—read the book, *Real Love—The Truth About Finding Unconditional Love and Fulfilling Relationships* (Go to http://www.gregbaer.com/book/book.asp).

ℬ ℭ*hapter Four* ℭℛ

Making the Bold Move

How to Have Great Dates and Fulfilling Relationships Every Time

This chapter is devoted to helping you find Real Love and the lasting, unconditionally loving relationships that inevitably follow. If your goal in dating is just to be entertained, or to get laid, I offer no criticism, but I do suggest that this book will not help you. There are many other sources eager to teach you how to manipulate people for approval, power, pleasure, and entertainment.

MEN AND WOMEN

When I talk about Real Love, many women wonder aloud, "Are there really men out there who are willing to talk about this subject? Aren't men just interested in sex, beer, and football?"

On the whole, men are more focused on sex than women are, but that superficial generalization doesn't help us understand the real differences between men and women, nor does it acknowledge that what men and women have in common is far more important than how they differ. When we realize that men and women share a primal need for Real Love, we can easily understand their behavior, and we can create enduring and easily-traveled bridges between the sexes.

As I have personally shared the principles of Real Love with thousands of people, I have concluded that although women are generally quicker to investigate Real Love, there is little or no difference between the sexes in their desire for it. Once men understand Real Love, they are just as diligent about acquiring it—and as willing to talk about it—as women are.

Where men and women differ most is in the forms of Imitation Love and Getting and Protecting Behaviors they use when they don't feel loved unconditionally. Influenced by a combination of genetics, hormones, and social norms, boys tend to use power and pleasure to fill their emptiness, while girls use praise and safety. Boys have a more aggressive inborn quality, which is also reinforced by social norms and expectations. It should be no surprise, then, to learn that boys tend to use attacking and lying as Getting and Protecting Behaviors, while girls are prone to use lying, acting like victims, running, and clinging.

> Men and women are much more alike than different. They share the common and essential need for Real Love.

We can see these male-female differences in many common situations. On an athletic team, for example, boys and men tend to value individual achievement. Although they also enjoy winning as a team, they often berate in a vicious way any member of the team whose individual performance is inferior. On a female team, however, team members tend to rally around and support a girl who is having a difficult time.

In the performance of a task, women generally try to make everyone feel good about their assignment and performance, whereas men are focused more on getting the job *done*. In conversation, most women are attentive to how the other person feels about the discussion, while most men are interested in getting their point across, and in proving that they're right. In all this, men are looking for a feeling of power, while women want to feel accepted.

Keep in mind that these are gross generalizations, and I understand that there are many men and women who deviate from these stereotypes. Fortunately, we don't need to dwell on the differences between men and women. It's far more productive to focus on the greatest need we all have—for Real Love.

FINDING REAL LOVE

In Chapter Three, we established that as long as we're pretending to be other than who we really are, we make it impossible to feel seen, accepted, and loved, as depicted again in this simple diagram:

Truth → Seen → Accepted → Loved

Only as I share with you who I really am—flaws and all—can I feel that you see who I am, accept me, and care about my happiness.

THE ROLE OF FAITH
IN TELLING THE TRUTH AND FINDING REAL LOVE

Even with the intellectual understanding that feeling Real Love requires that we tell the truth about ourselves, our first attempts at being truthful can be very frightening. Most of us learned in childhood to lie, and when we found that our lies often enabled us to minimize the painful criticism and rejection we could not tolerate, we continued this practice as adults. We have a hard time imagining that if we're open and honest now, we won't continue to experience the same pain we've known all our lives as people have criticized us, withdrawn from us, and felt disgusted by us.

Telling the truth about ourselves—especially in the beginning—requires faith. Faith is the act of moving into territory that is unknown to us. It means taking action when we can't predict the results. To be sure, exercising faith exposes us to the possibility of being hurt, but it also creates the opportunities for us to grow and multiply the joy in our lives.

Many of us are paralyzed by the risk of exposing ourselves to others, but it can be helpful to critically examine the realities of that risk. If you *don't* tell the truth about yourself to another person, what are the odds that you will ever feel unconditionally accepted by him or her? *Zero.* As long as you hide who you are, you cannot feel unconditionally seen, accepted, or loved. Now let's suppose that you tell the truth to someone, and we arbitrarily propose that the odds of that person accepting you are only 30%. Thirty percent is still a *lot* more than zero. In short, the real risk of being truthful with others about who we are is negligible. If we lie, we're doomed. If we're truthful, at least we create the *possibility* of feeling loved.

Truth → Seen → Accepted → Loved
Only as you share with others who you really are
—flaws and all—can you feel unconditionally
loved. Telling the truth initially requires great
faith.

Picture a farmer walking into a field with a bag of seeds on his shoulder. Imagine that he pulls a single seed out of the bag and says to himself, "You know, this seed might not grow. I'd hate to take the risk of it not growing, so I think I'll just stick it in my pocket instead." He pulls out a second seed and says the same thing. What kind of crop will this farmer get? A pocket full of seeds.

The only way a farmer can learn which seeds will grow is to plant them. As he does so, he takes the risk that some might not grow, but he also finds out which seeds *will* grow, and that's all that matters. If he plants all the seeds he has, and months later he's looking at a field full of waving grain, will it matter to him that some of the seeds didn't grow? Of course not.

Similarly, it doesn't matter how many people *don't* love you. What matters is that you find those who do, and that is possible only as you plant the seeds of who you really are in the hearts of those you meet. You will be richly rewarded by the crop you harvest.

TELL THE TRUTH TO WHOM

I am *not* suggesting that you rush out and start spilling your guts to everyone you know. That would just be too scary—for you and for them. Remember that the primary purpose of telling the truth about yourself is to create opportunities for you to feel seen, accepted, and loved. The term I apply to those people who are capable of accepting and loving you when you are truthful is *wise men* and *wise women*, or sometimes just *wise men*. The term *wise man* comes from a story found in Chapter Three of *Real Love—The Truth About Finding Unconditional Love and Fulfilling Relationships*. I suggest the following guidelines as you choose people to participate in your initial truthtelling experiments:

- Actively look for people who exhibit some capacity for Real Love.

- Be aware of your expectations.

- Avoid the potential for unnecessary injury.

- Don't tell the truth to people who would be injured by it.

- Choose faith over fear.

Now let's examine each of these guidelines in greater detail.

Actively Look for People Who Exhibit Some Capacity for Real Love

Imagine that you're in a large room filled with people. I approach you and give you an assignment to learn from these people as much as you can, in thirty minutes or less, about how to rope a calf. Contemplating how you might accomplish this task, several approaches come to mind. You could:

- Take a nap in the middle of the room, hoping that someone with a knowledge of calf roping will wake you up and give you the information you need.

- Stand in the middle of the room and listen to the conversations close by, hoping that calf roping will be among the topics discussed.

- Wander through the room, randomly selecting people to ask about their knowledge of calf roping.

- Interview the only two men wearing cowboy hats and boots, each of whom has a coil of rope in his right hand.

Although it's possible that all of these approaches could produce the desired result, you obviously want to choose the one that is most efficient. The passive approaches—the first two—are less likely to be successful than the active ones. Of the second two choices, your chances of success are much higher if you select candidates on the basis of obvious indicators (hats, boots, and rope).

Similarly, in the process of finding Real Love, an active approach is far more productive than a passive one. If you sit on your backside, hoping to be knocked over by a tidal wave of love, you could be in for a long wait. If, on the other hand, you actively seek people out and create opportunities for them to see you, you'll greatly increase the likelihood that you'll be loved. You'll further increase your chances of success if you choose people who demonstrate evidence that they possess the Real Love you seek.

Because Getting and Protecting Behaviors are only a reaction to a deficiency of Real Love, an absence of those behaviors is a strong indication of the presence of Real Love. People who feel unconditionally loved—and are therefore capable of loving you—simply don't have a *need* for Getting and Protecting Behaviors. As you look for people to see, accept, and love you, therefore, look for people who:

- Don't often get angry

- Usually don't complain and whine about people and circumstances

- Take responsibility for their mistakes, rather than making excuses and blaming others

- Can maintain a healthy eye contact with you

- Are generally kind to others, especially to those who are weaker

- Allow others to make their own decisions, rather than constantly trying to control them

- Don't avoid social interaction

- Don't constantly fish for compliments

- Don't engage in self-promotion and self-aggrandizement

- Don't try to control the conversation

- Don't have to be right all the time

- Are not overly complimentary or self-deprecating

- Have expressed some approval of you in the past, even while you were making a mistake

- Seem open-minded about political and social issues, and about individual lifestyles

- Ask questions and really seem to be interested in the answers

- You feel at ease with when you're being yourself

- Usually view people and circumstances in a positive light

- Have a good relationship with their children

It's not realistic to look for people who are perfectly loving all the time, but you can find those who possess a reasonable assortment of the qualities above. As you know what to look for, people with Real Love to share will become as obvious as a man wearing a cowboy hat and boots.

You can learn much more about identifying loving people in the two books, *Real Love—The Truth About Finding Unconditional Love and Fulfilling Relationships*, and *The Wise Man—The Truth About Sharing Real Love.*

Be Aware of Your Expectations

If the mailman didn't give you a kiss as you left the house for work in the morning, would you be offended? Of course not. If, on the other hand, your spouse or intimate partner consistently ignored you as you left the house each day, your reaction would likely be more intense. The difference? Expectations. With some people, your expectations of acceptance, attention, affection, and appreciation are much greater, and that is the case for one or more of a variety of reasons:

- You've given your own time and attention to that person, so you've determined—often unconsciously—that he or she "owes" you.

- According to social norms, that person occupies a

position in your life that *requires* him or her to care about you: spouse, parent, teacher, sibling, and other family members.

- He or she has promised to love you: parent, spouse. When people make promises to us, we tend to hold them to their commitments.

- You've determined that since someone knows you well, he or she should know what you need.

- Because of social norms, you expect a man or woman to behave in certain ways: pay for the date, open doors, and so on.

- Because of past experiences with others of the same sex, you have expectations of this partner. If other women have consistently given you sex, for example, you may expect the same from the woman you're with now. If other men have been consistently deferential, you may expect that kind of behavior from all men.

- That person occupies a social, emotional, familial, occupational or other position such that his or her acceptance *counts* more. If your boss, for example, is exceptionally competent, respected, and articulate, it's likely that his or her acceptance would be more valued by you. If you lack sufficient Real Love, you would have a greater *need* for the approval of that person, and would therefore be likely to *expect* it.

If you're like most of us, you already have a lifetime of not feeling loved unconditionally, which has led to the chronic conditions of emptiness and fear. In order to change those feelings, you need to get all the Real Love you can, and you need to be somewhat cautious about telling the truth about yourself to a boss or parent, for example, where your expectations would likely be high, because then if they're not met, you could be crushed, tearing open old emotional wounds.

Avoid the Potential for Unnecessary Injury

Imagine that you're seven years old, and you're learning to ride a bicycle. It's unavoidable that you'll make mistakes— wobbling, weaving, and probably an occasional fall. Although you can't avoid making mistakes, you *can* avoid making them in circumstances that would be *unnecessarily* harmful. You would not, for example, want to make your first attempts at riding a bike on an interstate highway, or on a busy downtown street, or in the aisles of a department store. Why choose such places to learn—where mistakes could result in damage to property or even your life—when you can practice in the relative safety of your own yard or driveway?

Similarly, although rejection and discomfort are unavoidable in the process of your telling the truth about yourself, you can avoid *unnecessarily* damaging situations. It would not be wise, for example, to initially expose everything about your personal life to your co-workers, where the consequences could be destructive to your career. Remember that you don't need the unconditional love of any particular person or group of people, so why choose a group where rejection and misunderstanding have an unnecessarily high price?

Eventually, as you feel more loved unconditionally, you'll find that you can be honest in more and more situations, including where you work. That feeling of security, however, builds only over significant periods of time.

Don't Tell the Truth to People Who Would Be Injured by it

In the process of telling the truth about yourself and feeling loved, it would be unloving to disregard the effect of what you're saying on the people who are listening. As many people come to an understanding of Real Love, for example, they realize they were not loved unconditionally by their parents—which has been true for the vast majority of us. Some of those people experience a compulsion to share this observation with their parents, failing to realize that very few parents are willing to have this conversation, and could only be hurt by it.

Sharing *some* of our mistakes with our children can be healthy, but some truths can only be frightening and hurtful to them. In addition, we should never tell children the truth about ourselves for the purpose of their loving *us*. That is an intolerable responsibility and burden to place on a child. You can learn a great deal more about parenting in the book, *Real Love in Parenting—A Simple and Powerfully Effective Way To Raise Happy and Responsible Children.*

Putting it All Together

Let's summarize what we've said about increasing the efficiency of finding Real Love. It's usually not wise to begin your truthtelling efforts with your parents, ex-spouses, co-workers, and children. Instead, pick a few friends, the ones who appear to be most accepting. Remember that you're looking for genuine acceptance not sympathy, which will not make you feel loved.

Telling the truth to a date is a great opportunity to be seen, but usually this is not productive until you feel loved enough by others—your friends and family, for example—that you can talk to a date without having expectations for acceptance. Because most of us approach a date with huge expectations, I recommend that you acquire considerable experience with feeling Real Love before you practice truthtelling with a date. More about that shortly.

Choose Faith over Fear

Although I have offered above some cautions about finding people to be honest with, my overall recommendation is that following the path of faith is far more productive than being frozen by fear. Have faith that you *will* find people capable of accepting and loving you. Never insist that any one person love you—we'll discuss that later in the chapter—but you *can* expect that if you tell the truth over and over, you will find the Real Love you need. If you listen too intently to your fears, you'll be paralyzed. Although hiding and running will somewhat limit the rejection you experience, with those behaviors you'll also eliminate any possibility of loving relationships.

For more on faith, see the section on faith earlier in this chapter, as well as Chapter Four of *Real Love—The Truth About Finding Unconditional Love and Fulfilling Relationships.*, and Chapter Six of *The Wise Man—The Truth About Sharing Real Love.*

HOW TO TELL THE TRUTH

When I first describe telling the truth about ourselves, many people imagine lying on a couch and talking to a psychoanalyst. That's not at all what I'm talking about. Telling the truth about yourself should be a natural, casual experience. You don't need to start off with the most intimate, frightening details of your life. Just tell the truth about the mistakes, flaws, fears, and Getting and Protecting Behaviors you encounter every day. Following are several examples of what you could say initially about yourself to friends:

- "Yesterday I really got mad at my brother. I wanted to blame him for my anger, but I'm beginning to realize that other people never 'make' me angry. Anger is a choice I make."

- "My boss asked me who screwed up a recent order that went out, and I blamed everybody but myself. The truth is, I could have done several things to make that order right, but I didn't admit any of that. Now I'm feeling a little guilty about it."

- "I've been reading a book called *Real Love*, and I'm learning a lot about why I behave the way I do. Would you be interested in reading my copy?"

- "My boyfriend didn't want to take me out a few nights ago, and I whined about it, which only made him feel guilty. And then we avoided each other all evening. I ruined a perfectly good evening."

- "My mother asked me to spend the weekend with her. I agreed to do that, even though I really didn't want to, and then I was grouchy the whole weekend. It was all my fault. I just should have told her I didn't want to come that weekend."

- "I had a real conflict with another employee at work this week. I made a fool of myself, actually. It would have gone quite differently if I hadn't been focused on controlling the situation, trying to make it all go my way. I was thinking about what *I* wanted, instead of thinking about what would have been best for everyone involved."

- "My girlfriend wasn't ready when I went to pick her up Friday, and I really got irritated. True, she's often late—which is her problem—but it was my anger that ruined the evening, not her being late."

- "Last week my boss told me something I did wrong, but I argued with him instead of listening. Then later I avoided him around the office, just to show him how annoyed I was with him. Pretty childish of me, really."

- "I went on a date last week that went poorly, because I was more interested in impressing her than getting to know her. I've realized that I can be pretty dishonest and selfish with my dates."

- "I've started to realize that I date women based solely on how they look, or what I expect them to do for me. I need to look for women who are interested in an honest relationship, and who can love me for who I am."

- "When I don't get what I want, I get upset and act like a victim. Sometimes I even cry to manipulate people into doing what I want. It was pretty embarrassing when I realized that I act just like my mother did."

Notice that none of these admissions is especially intimate or frightening, nor do they involve the use of psychological language or words unfamiliar to most people. You will still find, however, that some people have no interest whatever in a truthful discussion about you—but so what? Keep trying, and you *will* find those who are fascinated to learn about you. As you find such people, you can become increasingly direct with them in the language you use, especially if they've read the *Real Love* book. You can begin to describe Getting and Protecting Behaviors—and your use of Imitation Love—more clearly. For example:

- "When I'm around people I don't know, I get nervous that they won't like me, so I get real quiet. I'm a runner."

- "When my boyfriend doesn't give me something I want, I sulk. I act like a victim, and then sometimes he caves in and does what I want. I may win in the short term, but my acting like a victim isn't helping our relationship at all."

- "I'm beginning to see that at work I use anger as a Getting Behavior. When I'm angry, people feel intimidated, and then they're more likely to do what I want."

- "When I'm in a gathering of people, I like to dominate the conversation with stories about myself. I tend to exaggerate them, so I'll look good."

- "I'm beginning to see that I shop a lot because I'm hoping it will make me feel happier. It's just Imitation Love."

- "The other day I was on a date, and the guy was looking at other women. I got angry at him, but later I realized I was trying to control him. I was wrong to do that. He has the right to do whatever he wants, and I don't have the right to control him. I don't have to keep dating him, but I don't get to control him."

- "I dress provocatively on dates so that men will like me. But I'm really lying about who I am, and I'm ensuring that I won't feel genuinely accepted."

- "I had a confrontational situation with my boss yesterday, and rather than do what was needed to solve the problem, I got on the Internet and planned a personal vacation. I was running."

- "When I get bored, I tend to have 'adult' fantasies, and I go to the mall to fantasize about the women who walk by."

- "I'm an adrenaline junky. I love to take risks for the thrill of it. I go skydiving and skindiving because I feel like I've missed out on a lot in life, and I need the excitement."

- "In most social situations, I really tend to withdraw, staying at the edge of the room. I'm afraid people won't like who I am."

- "Since I was a teenager I thought no one would care enough about me to date me unless I had sex with them. So lots of times now I've traded sex for the Imitation Love I could get from guys."

- "I've had a long series of relationships over the past 12 years. I usually get discouraged, give up and withdraw when my partner disappoints me and doesn't live up to my expectations. Now I realize that many of my expectations are completely unreasonable."

You'll find many more examples of truthtelling—as well as explanations of it, and suggestions about how to respond to it—in:

- *Real Love—The Truth About Finding Unconditional Love and Fulfilling Relationships*

- *The Real Love Companion—Taking Steps Toward a Loving and Happy Life*

- *The Wise Man—The Truth About Sharing Real Love*

Getting Fed as Often as Possible

On many occasions, I have received calls from people who have said, "I tried this Real Love stuff, and it just doesn't work."

I usually respond by asking, "How often are you talking to people—by phone and in person—who are capable of loving you unconditionally?" In every case, they're not making much effort to get the love they need.

Getting Real Love is just as important as eating and breathing. If you want to experience real emotional and spiritual health, you need to get all the Real Love you can find—preferably every day. Call or meet every day with friends who can accept and love you as you tell the truth about your mistakes, flaws, and fears. You can't get too much love.

Participating in a Loving Group

The people who make the best progress in feeling Real Love are those who participate in Loving Groups, where people get together for the conscious purpose of practicing telling the truth and loving one another. Groups are meeting weekly all across the country, and the results are dramatic. To learn more about how to form such a group, and how to make it work, read:

- *Real Love—The Truth About Finding Unconditional Love and Fulfilling Relationships*

- *The Real Love Companion—Taking Steps Toward a Loving and Happy Life*

- *The Wise Man—The Truth About Sharing Real Love*

As you share what you're learning with friends, you'll naturally gather people who are willing to participate in a

Loving Group. Or you could initially ask people just to read the *Real Love* book together—a book club. As people discuss the principles of the book, they often begin to tell the truth about themselves naturally.

THE EFFECT OF FEELING REAL LOVE

We feel empty and afraid—and we use Getting and Protecting Behaviors—only because of a lifetime of not feeling sufficient Real Love. The people around us told us repeatedly—though almost always unintentionally—that they loved us less when we didn't do what they wanted. From these people who literally taught us the nature of the world we came to believe that we were not worth loving. Before we can eliminate the effects of that awful message, we must experience Real Love consistently for a significant period of time.

> Once you have sufficient Real Love from friends, family, and others, you'll feel like you have twenty million dollars all the time, and then you won't have a desperate need for the two dollars any one person will or will not give you in any given moment.

As we persist in exposing ourselves to the unconditional love of others, eventually we fill up with the twenty million dollars we always lacked. With sufficient Real Love, our emptiness and fear disappear, and then our Getting and Protecting Behaviors simply have no function. They disappear because they are no longer needed.

With Real Love, we enter into relationships with a desire not just for what we can get for ourselves but with a desire to love others. Under those conditions, healthy and mutually rewarding relationships become possible.

The Need for Real Love *Before* You Start Dating

When people are trying to lose weight, they're often told not to go shopping for food while they're hungry, a time when they're much more likely to buy foods incompatible with their new, healthy goals. Similarly, when you don't have sufficient Real Love—when you're empty and afraid—you're virtually certain to use Getting and Protecting Behaviors, which temporarily make you feel better but are incompatible with the Real Love and happiness you seek. When you're empty, you'll tend to settle for the Imitation Love—the emotional junk foods—that other people are willing to give you. Under those conditions it is virtually impossible to establish an unconditionally loving relationship with anyone.

Most of us date so we can find someone to "make" us happy. We go shopping while we're hungry and settle for anyone who will fill us up—however temporary that might be. But that's not a healthy way to find a partner. If you begin a relationship without sufficient Real Love, and your partner suffers from the same deficiency, you won't have anything to give one another, and when your expectations for happiness are not realized, you'll be terribly disappointed.

The secret to a great relationship is for both partners to enter into dating with enough Real Love that they're not empty and desperate to manipulate one another for Imitation Love. Each partner can then *add* to the love and happiness of the other, and a genuinely loving relationship becomes possible.

We all want to have a great relationship. We want the miracle that occurs when two people play a beautiful duet together, as I mentioned in Chapter One. Before you can participate in such a duet, however, you must first be able to play a solo instrument. Without that ability, you will only detract from the harmony. The secret to finding a loving partner is to *be* a loving partner yourself. You don't have to be perfectly loving, but you do need to be in the process of rising out of the pit of Getting and Protecting Behaviors, and not be completely captive to the distractions of Imitation Love.

Do not begin dating until you have enough Real Love that you are not consumed by emptiness and fear. If you fail to heed that advice, the foundation of your relationship is guaranteed to be rotten from the beginning.

We'll talk more about when to date—and when not to date—in Chapter Six.

THE PURPOSE OF DATING

Dating has two primary purposes:

- To practice sharing who you are with others

- To find people who are capable of being truthful, and who have a sincere interest in learning to love unconditionally

Some people suggest a third purpose—just to have fun—but on the whole, having fun without telling the truth and without Real Love tends to become a pursuit of Imitation Love. Two people who remember the real purposes of dating, on the other hand, will have fun while doing almost anything.

In this section we'll discuss the first purpose—telling the truth about ourselves—while in Chapter Five, we'll talk about how to find people who have an interest in telling the truth, and in learning to love unconditionally.

Telling the Truth on a Date

Imagine that after you place your order at a restaurant, the waiter brings you only a *photograph* of the food you ordered. Certainly you could enjoy the beauty of the pictures, but your physical hunger would remain unsatisfied. Similarly, on a date you could fill yourself up with the Imitation Love that is always readily available, but to settle for Imitation Love instead of Real Love is like choosing a picture of food instead of eating a real meal. Moreover, you'll never enjoy the latter until you begin to share who you really are with people. On a date, if you withhold the truth about yourself, you might as well stay home and simply send digitally enhanced photographs of yourself to your partner.

Being truthful on a date is so important that I want to emphasize it with a story. Once there was a swan who began a quest for the most beautiful mate possible. One day he spotted a peacock on the shore—a female peacock is actually called a peahen—and instantly he fell in love. Surely this was the most beautiful creature he had ever seen. Leaving the lake where he'd always lived, he courted the peacock, who at first paid him little attention. The swan, however, learned to strut and cry like a peacock, and he even gathered peacock feathers off the ground and glued them all over his body.

The hen was attracted to him and agreed to be his mate. As with any relationship, of course, there were problems. Because the swan found it difficult to eat with his bill what peacocks eat with their beaks, he became thinner and thinner. With his webbed feet, he also had difficulty perching in the limbs of trees at night, an easy task for the peacocks with their curved, grasping feet. Finally, exhausted and weak, he lost his perch in the middle of the night, fell to the ground, and was eaten by a large dog.

Although the absurdity of a swan imitating a peacock is obvious, most of us participate in similarly destructive deceptions all the time, as illustrated in the following story about Dave, a man who'd experienced little success in dating. One day at a singles bar, Dave decided to speak in an Australian accent. Instantly, women were attracted by the novelty of talking with someone from "down under," and he experienced more success in meeting women than he'd ever known. Encouraged by this, he continued his deception and actually moved in with a girl who thought he was Australian. She soon discovered, however, that he was not who he pretended to be—in many ways, not just his nationality—and she became disappointed and irritated. Eventually, she left him.

Although this example seems especially laughable, it's not so different from what most of us do in the process of finding a partner. We may not fake an accent. We may not consciously lie about ourselves, but we nonetheless change our feathers in many other ways.

It's tempting to put your best foot forward in the process of attracting a partner, but the results are almost always harmful. I'm not saying you should do nothing at all to enhance your image. I'm not saying you should go straight from slopping the hogs to meeting a date for dinner, but you do need to be cautious about how you attract a partner. The more you emphasize your positive qualities, while minimizing your mistakes, flaws, and fears, the more likely it is that you're portraying yourself in a false way. Do you really want a relationship based on lies? We'll shortly discuss how to deal with the fear of being rejected, and what we can do to enhance our image in healthy ways.

Dating has two primary purposes:

- To practice sharing who you are with others

- To find people who are capable of being truthful, and who have a sincere interest in learning to love unconditionally

---

Creating Your Online Profile

One of the most efficient ways you can meet people is on the Internet, and in Chapter Six, we'll discuss why that is. On the Internet, people first learn who you are through your profile, and with SoulMate you have a wonderful opportunity to reveal who you really are with the Real Love essay questions. With every truthful answer, you create a solid piece of the foundation upon which healthy relationships can be built. With every lie, no matter what form of Imitation Love you may get in the short term, you build into your foundation the flaws that will spell future disaster.

Let's discuss the essay questions on SoulMate.com, and how these create opportunities for you to build honest and loving relationships. I realize that answering these questions truthfully could be difficult for many. Our society teaches people to lie, so you may initially feel uncomfortable as you give honest answers here. You may be afraid that your honest will drive people away. It *will* drive some people away, but those are only people you wouldn't want as a partner anyway. So summon up your courage and tell the truth. The potential rewards are enormous: With your honesty, you'll be declaring that you're interested in an open, unconditionally accepting relationship, and you'll attract partners with a similar interest.

Describe a time you lied to a date, and why.

Most of us have represented ourselves less than honestly on dates. You'll find examples of lying in Chapter Three. Take the opportunity here to be open about some of the lies you've told, and be specific. If you gloss over what happened, or make excuses, you'll be declaring that you're still not capable of being honest. Be willing to laugh at your foolishness. Honesty is disarming and endearing.

Remember that admitting to a lie doesn't mean you're a bad person. You've lied only to win the approval of others, and to keep from looking bad—very much a part of the human condition.

You agree to meet your date at a restaurant at 7:30 p.m., but at the appointed time, he/she is not there. How long would you wait? At the end of the time you wait, as you're walking to your car, you run into your date on his/her way to the restaurant. What would you say to him/her about being late?

Don't try to look like Gandhi here. Don't say, "For my true love, I would wait forever." Say what you would really do and say in this situation.

How did your last two relationships end? How was any of that your fault?

When relationships end, we really don't want to be seen as the cause. We don't want to take responsibility for our mistakes. It can be especially difficult to admit your mistakes when you can so easily describe all the things your partner did wrong. The fact is, what your partner did wrong doesn't really matter. You can't control any of that. Focus instead on what *you* did. That's the only part you can change. Tell the truth about *you*. If you can point a finger only at the faults of past partners, your present partner can only conclude that your next target will be him or her.

Following are some examples of your telling the truth about yourself, specifically as you contributed to a failed relationship:

- "I kept looking at other women, and flirting. I knew it bothered her, but I did it anyway."

- "I kept trying to change him. My mother does the same thing to my father, and I swore I'd never do it to my own partner, but I still did it."

- "I couldn't make a commitment to the relationship. When things get too intimate, I tend to be a runner."

- "I was too demanding. The more time he spent with me, the more time I demanded. It got to the point where I was making him tell me where he went, and why he wasn't with me, all the time."

- "It's my anger that wrecked my last relationship. I get annoyed over the smallest things, and finally she couldn't take it anymore."

- "I was too jealous. After we'd been together for a few months, I didn't like it when he (or she) spent time with anybody but me."

- "I got scared. The more time we spent together, the more I could see that I wasn't ready for a longterm relationship. I ran."

- "I was too critical. When he/she did things I didn't like, I made way too many comments."

- "I let my kids get in the way. Whenever there was a choice between him/her and the kids, I chose the kids. Sure, my children are important, but over and over, I told my partner that he/she wasn't important."

- "I'm addicted to my job. I always put my career first, and he/she finally got tired of it."

- "I just didn't know how to have a relationship. I expected too much, and gave too little. The more I'm learning about relationships, the more I can see how selfish I was."

- "I kept holding inside what I really wanted to say most of the time, because I was afraid I would look stupid. My withdrawing made her crazy."

- "I got committed to my last new relationship too quickly, before I knew the man well enough to find out if he was right for me. Later on I regretted that I didn't get to know him much better before I got so deeply involved. That made it very painful to end the relationship."

On average, you have sex with a partner after how many dates? If your partner isn't interested in sex after that many dates, what do you usually do?

Many of us use sex as a form of Imitation Love, and we demand it of our partners, often in subtle ways. If you expect sex after a couple of dates, as a sign that your partner really cares about you, don't hide that fact. When you don't get the sex you expect, what do you do? Do you make demanding comments? Do you leave the relationship?

Describe something (or someone) that irritates you. Now describe what that irritation says about you.

Most of us are either irritated or at the edge of irritation, much of the time. A friend once said to me, "I don't think people are as irritated as you think." I responded, "Walk into any Wal-Mart, and cut in line." For most of us, irritation is only the slightest provocation away. Describing people and things that irritate us is relatively easy:

- People who are late
- Noisy neighbors
- People who don't know how to drive
- Demanding bosses
- Ingratitude
- Hypocrisy
- Parents
- Waiting in line
- The weather
- Red lights
- People who have more than 10 items in the express lane
- People who have no clue that they are in the way until you ask them to move
- People who let their child cry without making any attempt to see what the child wants

- People who think they can bring a truck in their carry-on luggage, and then try to shove it in the overhead bin

- People who don't keep their commitments

- People who chew with their mouths open

It's much harder to admit *why* these things and people irritate us. When you see anger as a Getting and Protecting Behavior, your anger begins to make much more sense. In the beginning, your realizations may not be flattering:

- "Every time my boss is a horse's butt, I take it personally. I don't mind that he's demanding and angry at everybody else in his life, but when it come to me, I expect that he'll suddenly be considerate. Crazy, huh?"

- "I get impatient with people pretty easily. When they inconvenience me, I really don't like it. I'm selfish."

- "I get angry pretty often at other drivers. It's ridiculous, but somehow I think everybody on the road should know that they're supposed to make my life easy."

- "When I do something for somebody, and they're not grateful, that really bugs me. Makes me realize that I don't really give gifts unconditionally. I expect something in return."

- "I'm angry that the weather doesn't submit a plan for my approval. How could it be so thoughtless as to inconvenience me?"

- "I get mad when other people hog a conversation. Don't they know that everyone is supposed to be paying attention to *me*?"

While on a date, you notice that your partner keeps looking at other men/women as they walk by. What would you say?

Do you get insanely jealous and angry?

Would you keep it to yourself, or would you express it openly? Do you sometimes look at other men/women yourself?

What do you fear most when you go out on a date?

Almost everyone is nervous on a date, especially a first date. "Nervous" is just a more socially acceptable way of saying "afraid." Other words we use to disguise our fear are *anxious*, *concerned*, *uneasy*, and *shy*.

We are afraid of so many things, and one of the best ways to lose our fears is to talk about them.

- "I'm afraid my date won't like me." Almost all of our fears are versions of, "I'm afraid I won't be loved."

- "I'm afraid I'll do something stupid." Why? Because again, if I do something stupid, I'm afraid I won't be liked/loved.

- "I'm afraid I'll find another loser, but I won't realize it until months later, after a painful break-up. I hate those."

- "I'm afraid I'll never find the right person for me."

- "I'm afraid that nobody's ever going to think I'm the right person for them."

- "I'm afraid he/she won't think I'm attractive."

- "I'm afraid he/she will think my career isn't very impressive."

- "I'm afraid to talk about my past sexual experiences."

- "I'm afraid that this guy/girl will be hiding something from me, and I won't be smart enough to sense that."

- "I'm afraid if I don't have sex, or at least act sexy, I'll never hear from the guy again."

- "I'm afraid my date will be really disappointed and hurt if I don't like him."

- "I'm afraid my date will think I'm boring so I work hard at entertaining him by being funny and smart."

- "I'm afraid my date is a phony, but I won't be able to figure that out."

- "I'm afraid he or she will think I'm weird."

Describe a moment in your life that still brings you pain as you think of it.

You don't have to discuss the most difficult moments in your life immediately. The purpose of this question is only to give potential partners an idea about your ability to be truthful. With that in mind, don't get distracted by the opportunity you have here to act like a victim. When most people are asked to describe a painful moment, they don't describe *themselves*; rather, they describe something that happened *to* them: a family death, a hurricane, a car accident, and so on. Who you are is determined by the choices you make, not by what happens *to* you. For that reason, take a deep breath and talk about the choices *you* have made.

- "When I dumped my last partner, I didn't really give him/her an explanation that made any sense. I know that was painful for him/her."

- "In college, I played a practical joke on my roommate that embarrassed him badly in front of a lot of people. I never did apologize for it."

- "On my mother's birthday, I was drunk and made a real ass of myself."

- "When my children misbehave, I get impatient pretty quickly, and then I start yelling. I know I'm hurting them, but I do it anyway."

- "At work, I'm pretty harsh when one of my co-workers screws up, and I know it makes him feel bad. I know I should quit it, but so far I haven't."

- "When my uncle died, I didn't attend the funeral. In fact, I didn't call, send a card, or send flowers. I know it was important to my aunt, but I still didn't do anything."

- "Last time my nephew came over to visit, I watched television almost the entire time. It was obvious he felt ignored, but I did what I wanted anyway."

- "I cheated on my last partner."

- "I did some cruel things to my younger brothers when we were growing up. I was empty and just didn't know any better, but still I have some moments of huge regret."

- "I lied on my dating profile. I don't really make $150,000/ year, but I wanted to attract someone who has money. And furthermore, I'm only 5'6" tall, not 5'8" but I know men like tall women."

What do you want most from a date?

Don't fake this. Don't say, "I want to work with my date on a plan for world peace"—unless you're dating a Miss America judge or the Secretary General of the United Nations. If you answer this question deceptively, you'll spend the rest of your relationship wondering why there's such a disparity between what you want and what you're getting. Also remember that with time and experience with the principles of Real Love, your answer to this question will change.

- "A companion. At this point, I'm not all that interested in a committed relationship, just somebody to have a good time with."

- "Sex."

- "I'm looking for a committed relationship."

- "A sense of humor."

- "Kindness."

- "Somebody I can be honest with, somebody who can accept me as I am, warts and all."

- "Somebody who enjoys the outdoors like I do."

- "Somebody I just hit it off with."

- "Somebody who can dance."

- "Somebody who can hold up their end of an interesting conversation on many topics."

How do you go about arranging the financial aspects of a date—who will be paying for what? Do you just assume that you or your date will pay for the whole thing? Do you talk about it? If you don't discuss this issue, why not?

- "I've never talked about it, so there's always this uncomfortable moment at the end of the date where we figure it out with body language, eye contact, and hints. I guess I should talk about it earlier in the date."

- "I was raised to believe that the man always pays for the date, but I'd be willing to talk about it."

- "I figure whoever *asks* the other person for the date is the one who pays, and so far that's worked out for me.

- "I always say to the guy ahead of time, 'I'd like to pay my way, if that's all right.' That way I don't feel any pressure, like I owe him anything."

- "I've always wanted to talk about it, but talking about money makes me very uncomfortable, so I avoid it by paying for the date myself."

- "Until we get to know one another better, I'd rather that we each paid our own way. It eliminates a feeling of obligation. Is that all right with you?"

- "I'd like to take you out for dinner—my treat this time. We can talk about paying for other dates later, if that's all right with you."

Describe a mistake you made recently at work.

- "I was supposed to get a piece of information from one of our clients before we had our next staff meeting, but I put it off till the last minute, and then the client didn't have time to get the information together before the meeting. When the boss asked for the information, I blamed the delay on the client.

- "I tend to live in a bit of crisis mode at work most of the time. I put off doing the things I don't like to do, so when they just *have* to be done, I rush around in a panic. This does not make for a peaceful work environment."

- "I snapped at one of my employees for misplacing a file. Later, I found it on my desk, under a pile of stuff, and I never told the employee that the mistake was mine.

- "I called in sick, when I was really out doing some errands."

- "I said some unkind things to a co-worker about another co-worker.

- "I said I forgot to clock in, when the truth was, I got to work half an hour late, and I didn't want that on my time card. So I lied, and got my supervisor to write in that I'd gotten there on time."

- "When the boss gave me an assignment I didn't like— mostly because it wasn't in my job description—I took as long as possible to do it, kind of to get him back for giving me that task in the first place.

- "I spent a fair amount of time yesterday playing games

on the Internet, when I should have been working. It was lazy and dishonest of me.

- "I often make personal long-distance calls from work, even though it's against company policy. I'm not being honest about that.

- "Sometimes I use company equipment and supplies for personal reasons.

- "Sometimes I do the least I can do at work, making other people tell me what to do, when I already know what I should be doing.

- "Yesterday I spent an hour at work playing games on the Internet, even though my boss was waiting for me to finish a project for him."

Describe a quality about yourself that isn't flattering.

- "I don't have good control over my temper.

- "I have a pretty strong need to be right."

- "I have a tendency to speed when I drive. Three tickets in the past year alone.

- "I'm not very good at managing money. I keep overdrawing my checking account."

- "I tend to lead men on sexually, but then I want them to keep their hands off me.

- "When I'm in a group, I often take over the conversation. People have told me about it, but I still do it."

- "I'm getting a bit flabby and out of shape.

- "I can really be sarcastic at times. It's not kind.

- "Sometimes I laugh to cover up how nervous I am.

- "I often like to prove that I'm the smartest person in the group.

- "I take things too personally."

Your date tells you that your position on a particular political or social issue is "stupid," and it's obvious that he/she is irritated. How do you deal with that?

- "I get real quiet, and don't offer another opinion that evening.
- "I explain my position again."
- "I get offended and say something unkind in return."
- "I show him/her how it's really *his* position that's stupid."
- "I change the subject of the conversation.
- "I explain that I don't appreciate being called stupid."
- "I say, 'Yo mama!'"
- "I use it against him or her later in the date."
- "I get up and leave."
- "I realize that his or her opinion has nothing to do with me, and simply note my date's tendency to be critical, or to insist on being right."
- "I remember that issue and simply avoid it in the future."
- "I make a joke about it."

By the end of your first date—which you arranged by e-mail— you've decided not to pursue a second date with your partner. When he/she asks, "Could I have your phone number?" what do you say in return?

- "Sure you can." Then you screen all your calls with your answering machine, and you never pick up when he/she calls

- "No."

- "Of course," and then you give him/her a fake number

- "I've enjoyed myself tonight, but I'd rather not take it any farther."

- "Can I have your number instead? Then I can call *you*.

- "Are you familiar with the term, 'a snowball's chance'?"

- "I'd love to give it to you, but I just moved in, and I can't remember it.

- "I don't think so. Not your fault. I'm just looking for something else—all my own quirks, not a deficiency in you."

What do you expect a lifelong partner to bring to a relationship with you?

- "A best friend."

- "Sex."

- "Willingness to make a commitment."

- "A sense of humor."

- "Kindness."

- "Somebody I can be honest with, somebody who can accept me as I am, warts and all."

- "Somebody I can do stuff with: hiking, camping, cycling.

- "Somebody who can help me as a parent."

- "A willingness to have children with me."

- "Financial independence."

- "Emotional stability."

> Telling the truth about yourself can be frightening, but the alternative is much worse.

Telling the Truth about Yourself on the First Few Dates

Even though honesty is an essential element of any meaningful date, telling the truth can still be a frightening experience. You'll be much better prepared to be truthful if on many previous occasions you have told the truth and experienced the unconditional acceptance of friends—as we discussed earlier. As you carry the love of friends with you into a date, your emptiness and fear will be much relieved, and then Getting and Protecting Behaviors become unnecessary.

How should you go about being truthful on a first or second date? For a start, you can use as a guide what is found in an earlier section of this chapter, "How to Tell the Truth." Some things about yourself—more intimate, private matters—are better shared after a relationship is more established: perhaps after the third or fourth date, or even later. In Chapter Six, we'll discuss how to handle those matters. Following are some additional truths you could share early in dating:

- "I get nervous on first dates. Do you?" If your date replies in the affirmative, you can both talk about what makes you nervous, that you're afraid you won't be liked.

- "I was going through my closet tonight to pick out something that looked good, but I decided I was more interested in wearing something that was comfortable. Trying to impress people is a lot of work, and I'm not sure I like the result."

- When he talks about football, you admit that you don't really know much about it.

- When she asks if you like children, you don't respond with what you know she wants to hear. You tell her the truth, even if it's not flattering. For example, you might say, "I don't mind being around them when they're well-behaved, but I must admit I get impatient when they're not."

- He talks about the books he's read, and you admit that you watch television more than you read.

- Instead of lying about all the advancement opportunities ahead of you in your career, you admit, "I'm not sure I want to work in a supervisory position. I don't know if I want the extra responsibility."

- "I'm pretty ignorant about politics. In fact, I haven't voted in years."

- "The gym? As you can see, I'd rather go to McDonald's."

- "I don't like to travel. I'd rather relax at home with a book or the television."

- "The closest I get to ethnic food is a trip to Taco Bell."

- "I don't drink anymore, and I'm afraid to tell people that, because then they often think I'm being narrow-minded, or that I'll criticize them for drinking. Lots of social functions revolve around drinking, so now I feel a little out of place."

- "Sometimes on dates, I have a couple of drinks early on, because that helps me eliminate some of my fears. I know it's artificial, but I still do it."

- "I don't get involved in politics—I really don't understand it."

Another way to introduce truthtelling on a date is to bring along a print-out of the answer you and your date gave to the SoulMate/RealLove essay questions above. Ask for (and give) clarification or amplification of the answers found on the website.

You could also come up with questions of your own. Don't pose the questions with the attitude that you're administering a test or an interrogation. You're just creating opportunities for both you and your date to get to know one another. Anyone who would resist such sharing would also be likely to resist overall honesty in a relationship.

WHAT IF YOUR DATE DOESN'T LIKE THE TRUTH ABOUT YOU?

When in doubt, tell the truth, right from the beginning. Sure, there will be some who won't like you—who will be scared off, never to be seen again. *So what?! Hallelujah!!*

Would you rather learn after thirty minutes together that the person you're with doesn't like you, or would you prefer arriving at that conclusion after ten years and three children? Is there any doubt whatever in your mind which of those two courses is the wiser? And yet we persist in trying to *get* our dates to like us, only to find out six months or years later that it was a huge mistake.

We need to recognize *early* in a relationship that it won't work, instead of trying to make a relationship where there isn't one. Do you really want a relationship with a guy or woman whose affection you have to *buy*? Do you want a relationship with someone you have to keep lying to, that *will* someday be disappointed in you when he or she learns the truth about you?

You lose nothing by telling the truth in the beginning. If someone rejects you, you just find out *now* what you would learn in the end anyway. Learning early is far more efficient.

I have met with hundreds of individuals who were engaged or living with a partner, and who have said, "The longer we're together, the less sure I am that we should stay together." In every case, they began their relationships based on lies, and it took them months, in many cases years to figure out that they weren't compatible. Some of these couples have been engaged for many years. It should be obvious that this is not an efficient way to find a partner.

Imagine that, on average, you date a new person once every two weeks. You become serious with one in ten of those people. Once you're serious, it takes you about a year before you figure out whether you could have a great relationship with that person. Ignoring the subtleties of statistics, in a period of eighteen months you might be able to meet thirteen people (having spent a year with one person).

Now imagine that you're honest with your dates from the beginning, and you look for the same quality in a partner. Again, you date a new person once every two weeks, but because you learn so much more about each person on the first date, you don't waste a year with any one of them. Now you're able to meet thirty-eight people in eighteen months—much more productive.

> If you tell the truth about yourself to the people you date, it's true that some won't like you. But *only* as you are truthful will you find those who accept and love you for who you really are.

Telling the truth is the way to go. We keep telling our lies only because we've never seen it done any other way. We simply can't imagine what a completely honest relationship would look like. Let me tell you what it looks like. If you keep telling the truth on first dates and in other areas of your life, you'll eventually attract people who will accept and love you for who you really are. You will experience the unbelievable freedom of being yourself all the time—no lies, no pretending, no working to please people, no worrying that somebody might not like you. You'll know what it's like to have people care about *your* happiness without you doing anything to earn it. There's no feeling like it in the world.

In Chapter 6, we'll talk about the advantages of dating online.

TWO KEYS TO GREAT RELATIONSHIPS

For great relationships, there are two keys to success:

- Tell the truth about yourself.

- Never try to get any one person or group of people to love you—or like you.

We've discussed the first key at length in this chapter. It's the second key—a principle quite unfamiliar to most of us—that we'll discuss in this section.

Most of us approach dating in the following way:

- We evaluate each person in the dating pool for how much Imitation Love he or she might give us.

- When we find someone who gives us as much Imitation Love as we give him or her—or more—we do our best to *get* that person to like us. (Sometimes we settle for someone simply because that partner agrees to accept as much Imitation Love as we give him or her, even though we don't get as much as we give.)

Getting other people to like us—with the way we look, what we say, what we do—is so common that we accept it as normal, even desirable. The instant, however, that you do anything to get someone to like you, you have made it impossible to feel loved unconditionally. If that person actually does give you their attention and affection, you can feel it only as a reward for your manipulations. You cannot feel it as a gift given unconditionally.

Rather than trying to *get* anyone to like you, the key is simply to let other people see who you really are, and *find out* who likes you. Under those conditions, whatever love you get will be received freely, unconditionally.

Let's look at the numbers. Suppose your goal is to win the affection of a potential pool of ten men or women. With your best efforts at appearance, speech, and behavior, you manage to earn the approval of six of those people. In truth, however, you now have the *unconditional* love of *no one*. Now suppose that you make no effort whatever to get any of those ten people to like you. You decide just to be yourself, and as a result only three of them like you. Although three may appear to be less than six, what you receive from those three is acceptance for who you really are—unconditional acceptance.

As a result of manipulating, you consistently get a *zero* % yield of Real Love. As a result of being honest, you get 30%, which is infinitely greater than zero.

Earlier in this chapter we talked about faith, and we compared telling the truth about yourself to a farmer planting seeds. You can find out who will love you unconditionally only as you simply plant the seeds of who you are. Some of those seeds won't grow, but the seeds that do grow have infinite worth. In the end, it doesn't matter how many people *don't* love you, only that you find those who *do*, and that can only happen as you share with others who you really are.

GETTING TO "NO" FASTER
OR
THE JOY OF REJECTION

Once you see the foolishness of ever trying to win conditional acceptance, and that finding Real Love can happen only after telling the truth about yourself, you'll want to be truthful about yourself with as many people as possible. A farmer doesn't get a big crop by being careful only to plant seeds that will grow. He gets a big crop by planting as many seeds as possible. Although he knows that some of them won't grow, he knows that many seeds will grow, and will produce an abundant harvest.

The more people who know who you really are, the more likely it will be that you will find people who love you unconditionally. In the process, it's unavoidable that some of those people will *not* like you, but so what? Those moments of rejection are unavoidable in your quest for those who will accept and love you.

On many occasions, people have approached me for advice about how to handle terrible relationships or engagements that have been going on for years. In each case, the relationship seemed to have a "great" beginning, founded on the abundance of Imitation Love. When the effects of Imitation Love wore off, the relationship foundered. For years, these people tried to revive a doomed relationship, with predictable results.

It's unavoidable that you will find people with whom you will not have an unconditionally loving relationship, but why in the world would you want to spend years of your life coming to that conclusion with each of those relationships? The real question, then, is not *whether* there will be moments of rejection, but *how long* you want those moments to last. The goal should not be to avoid rejection, but to move more quickly through those moments to get to the acceptance you seek. Your goal in dating should not be to avoid hearing *no* but to get to *no* more quickly.

Dating becomes an entirely different experience when we realize that lying will never really protect us in the long run. In fact, lying can only keep us feeling alone and unloved. When we really understand that, we realize that telling the truth about ourselves isn't risky. With truthtelling, there is only a *chance* we won't be loved. With lying, on the other hand, we're *guaranteed* not to feel loved.

One of the primary goals of dating is to learn more quickly that you do *not* want to have a relationship with the person you're with. If you tell the truth about yourself in the beginning, you will learn quickly whether the person you're talking to is a real possibility. If you lie, you won't learn that for a great deal longer.

> The goal of dating should not be to avoid rejection. It should be to move through rejections *faster*, so you can move onto relationships that can work.

If you tell the truth about yourself, and the man or woman you're talking to obviously isn't interested in you, *be grateful*. Be happy that you learned this early in the relationship, instead of months or years later. When somebody rejects who you are, don't be sad. Instead, say—at least to yourself—"Thank you. Thank you so much for saving me the time I could have wasted while figuring out that this relationship couldn't possibly work. Now I can move on."

In every young relationship, remember that the more time, money, emotion, and energy invested into a relationship, the harder it is to leave. It's usually wiser to cut your losses early.

Make it your goal in dating to gather *information* about your partners, rather than trying to make a relationship where a healthy one isn't possible. In ideal dating, two people would say, "This is who I am. Would you like to spend more time with me?"

Never Settle for Less than Gold

When I was a child, we lived within easy driving distance of an open-pit copper mine. To me, it was a huge playground of winding roads as wide as football fields, layers of brightly-colored minerals, enormous machinery, and a hole as big as the Grand Canyon. But my favorite thing was the gold. On my first visit, I found gold nuggets all over the sides of the road. It was a dream come true, and I took home as much of it as I could carry.

Then I learned it wasn't gold but pyrite, a shiny, gold-colored metal called fool's gold. But I kept it anyway, and each night I wished that by morning it would turn into gold. For days I got out of bed, emptied the nuggets onto my bed from a cloth bag where I kept them, and was deeply disappointed when I saw that during the night they hadn't transformed themselves into gold. They never did.

I could have persisted for years in my wishing, but that pyrite would never have turned into gold. You can't get gold by making it out of something else. If you want it, you have to find it where it is.

> Never settle for less than Real Love in a relationship. Anything else is a waste of your life.

Most of us try to find a partner in a way similar to that which I employed as a child to find gold. We locate what seems to be an attractive candidate, and then we try to make him or her into what we want. Of course, that leads only to frustration and pain. If we want a marriage filled with Real Love, we need to *find* a partner capable of participating in such a relationship, instead of trying to change the partner we find and *make* him or her capable of giving us what we want.

When we understand this, we'll know the answer to the question I often hear—with many variations—from single people involved in a relationship: "How do I *get* him (or her) to pay more attention to me, to be more thoughtful, to make a commitment to me, or to love me?" The answer is, you *don't*. You don't attempt to *get* a potential spouse to do anything. You simply *look* for a partner with the characteristics—we'll talk about what they are in chapter Five—you believe will contribute to a loving and happy relationship.

You can certainly *hope* that each person you meet, each person you date, *could* be that partner who will add to the Real Love in your life, but you cannot have an *expectation* of any single person. The difference between those two attitudes is enormous. A great relationship is the mutual offering and acceptance of unconditional love, not an exchange of any kind. If we exchange love, the transaction will inevitably become unsatisfying, unfair, and often bitter.

THE TRUTH ABOUT RELATIONSHIPS

A relationship is a natural result of people making independent choices. Let's examine two important phrases in that statement: "natural result" and "independent choices."

If you mix blue paint and yellow paint, the result will be green—every time. Green is a natural, unavoidable result of mixing blue and yellow. You don't get green because you *want* it, or because you work at it. Green just happens when you mix those two colors.

Similarly, a relationship is not what we want, or what we try to make it. It simply results from the independent choices made by each of the parties participating in it. You can't work on a relationship. You can, however, learn how to independently make choices that lead to more Real Love in your life, and *that* will change your relationships significantly.

Learn more about relationships in *Real Love—The Truth About Finding Real Love and Fulfilling Relationships*.

The Law of Choice

Now the second phrase, "independent choices." Easily the most important principle in relationships is the Law of Choice, which states that "Everyone has the right to say and do what he or she chooses"—even when you don't like it.

This principle seems obvious, but every time we become irritated at other people, we are declaring that we don't believe in the Law of Choice. We're saying that other people may make their own choices and mistakes until they inconvenience *us*.

It's tempting to want to control our partners—in many respects life would be more convenient, at least temporarily—but imagine the results if we actually succeeded. Everyone would become nothing more than puppets in our hands. Our partners could never be happy in that condition, nor could we, because they would become nothing more than objects in our control—and then we would be alone.

The Three Choices:
Live with it and Like it
Live with it and Hate it
Leave it

Just as other people have the right to make their own choices, so do we, and we always have a choice. So often we believe that we are trapped in a relationship, or in a situation, and that is rarely true, as illustrated by the following story about Cheryl and her boyfriend, Jim. Cheryl explained to me that once they had enjoyed a great relationship, but now they were growing apart. They used to spend all their time together, but now Jim was avoiding her.

"No matter how I push him," said Cheryl, "he still seems distant all the time."

"Sounds to me," I said, "like you're trying to change him, and he doesn't like that. You have no right to change him."

"I'm not trying to change him," said Cheryl. "I just want him to spend more time with me."

"Which would involve changing him."

"So what can I do?" asked Cheryl. "It sounds like I'm trapped in a situation I don't like."

"You're never trapped. You always have choices." Then I explained to Cheryl that she had three choices:

Live with it and like it
Live with it and hate it
Leave it

We examined them in turn. First, live with it and hate it. "Right now," I said, "you're choosing to live in a relationship where you're resentful and frustrated. Are you happy?"

"No," she said.

How often have we persisted in dealing with a situation or a relationship we resented? How many times has that ever made us happy? Not a single time, and yet we keep doing it. We need to discard this never-productive choice as foolish, which I explained to Cheryl.

"Are you ready to leave him?" I asked.

"No."

"Then we're left with 'Live with it and like it.'"

"How can I like it when he withdraws from me?"

"Everything changes when you see things differently, and when you have more Real Love in your life."

I explained how they had begun their relationship on the basis of Imitation Love, neither of them aware of what they were doing. When Jim felt the positive effects of Imitation Love wearing off, he began to withdraw from Cheryl (running), unfairly blaming her for the decrease in his happiness. When Cheryl sensed his running, she began to act like a victim, attack, and cling, all of which were guaranteed to accelerate his running. They were both caught in a destructive pattern of Getting and Protecting Behaviors.

"When you see that Jim is only trying to protect himself," I said, "that will greatly diminish your irritation at him. Then you need to begin the process of telling the truth about yourself, so you can get the Real Love that will change your relationship."

"But Jim doesn't have any more Real Love in his life than I do. What good will it do to tell him the truth about myself?"

"It might not do any good," I said, "but you'll never know until you try. Tell him that you've been demanding and selfish, and ask his forgiveness."

"*I've* been selfish? What about *him*?"

"He's being selfish, too, but you can't change him, remember? You can only change your own choices."

Cheryl did go to Jim, and she told him the truth about herself. When she returned to talk to me, however, she wasn't happy. "When I tried to talk to him, he just pulled away even more. Now what?"

"Do you want to leave this relationship?"

"No, I don't think so," she said. "Not yet."

"Then get more of the Real Love you need from people who actually have it. Discuss the *Real Love* book with some friends, and identify those who would be willing to be wise men and women for you. As you fill up with their love, you'll be able to take that back to your relationship with Jim, and then we'll see if that makes a difference."

Cheryl began to talk about Real Love with several friends, and she was surprised at the difference it made in her. As she filled up with twenty millions dollars (Chapter Three), she no longer had to fuss and fume at Jim over the two dollars she didn't get from him here and there. Instead, she began to share with him the love she had received from others—she extended her hand to him while he was drowning (Chapter Three)—and Jim responded to her unconditional love. As he got out of the pool, he no longer had a need to protect himself, and their relationship improved dramatically.

In some cases, it's wiser to leave a relationship, which we'll discuss in Chapter Nine.

In every relationship, and in every situation, you always have three choices:

Live with it and like it
Live with it and hate it
Leave it

You can learn more about the Law of Choice in the books, *Real Love—The Truth about Finding Unconditional Love and Fulfilling Relationships*, and *The Wise Man—The Truth About Sharing Real Love*.

THE LAW OF EXPECTATIONS

The Law of Expectations states, "We never have the right to expect other people to do anything for us." This is obvious when we understand the Law of Choice. If other people have the right to make their own choices, how dare we expect them to change their choices for our own convenience?

Every time we get angry at another person, we're proving that we have expectations. We expect them to behave in a certain way, and when they don't, we're angry that we can't control them.

Expectations are wrong because they violate the Law of Choice, and because they simply don't work. Imagine that I expect you to give me a dozen roses for my birthday, but you give me nine. Guess what I'll be thinking of? The three you didn't give me. With my expectations alone, I destroyed the possibility of feeling your gift. If, on the other hand, I have no expectations at all, I'll be thrilled even if you give me only one rose. Ironically, if I expect twelve roses, and you actually give me twelve, I won't feel loved and fulfilled. I'll feel only the brief satisfaction that comes from having an order filled, an enormous step down from feeling loved.

The instant I expect something from you, I destroy any possibility that I will feel loved unconditionally. Expectations are that harmful. How, then, can we eliminate them?

The first step is simple and intellectual. When you understand the Law of Choice, you realize that you have no right to interfere with the choices of others. You have no right to expect that other people will make only those choices that are convenient to you.

Intellectual understanding alone, however, is rarely enough to eliminate our expectations, and that's because we are so needy, because we don't have enough of the one element—Real Love— most essential to our happiness. Knowing that our neediness is the cause of our expectations can help us identify the way to eliminate them.

Imagine that you're out in the middle of the desert, lost and starving. A man who is obviously well-fed walks by with a large sandwich in his hand. What is your reaction? Understandably, you immediately ask him to share his sandwich with you. If he refuses, your request would almost certainly escalate into a plea or demand (remember, you're starving, not just a bit hungry). You would have an *expectation* of this man to share with you what he has.

Now picture a scene where again you're out in the middle of the desert, but this time you've just eaten a large meal, there is a huge table beside you that is groaning under the weight of the food piled on it, and you have a Humvee at your disposal to quickly get you out of the desert. Again a man walks by with a sandwich in his hand. Would you react to him in the same fashion you did the first time? Of course not. This time you wouldn't have huge expectations that he would share with you. You might not even notice the sandwich.

As you fill up with Real Love from those who have it to give, you'll feel complete and satisfied, after which you will naturally and effortlessly begin to lose the expectations that any one person or group of people should give you what you want in any given moment. Without the burden of expectations, you'll find it so much easier to begin and to build relationships.

ℰℴ *Chapter Five* ℭℛ

Spotting the Gold and
Avoiding the Rocks

What to Look For—
And What to Avoid—In a Partner

On many occasions I've been asked, "So you're saying that if we get enough Real Love in our lives, we could love everyone. If that's the case, why bother to date and find the 'right' person? If we can love everyone, why not just marry the next person we run into?"

THE CRITERIA FOR SELECTING A PARTNER

In Chapter Two, I said this:

> Although we can certainly learn to accept and love everyone without their doing anything for us—the definition of Real Love—that doesn't mean we won't find some people more enjoyable to be around.

> Although you can learn to unconditionally love everyone, that doesn't mean you want to date or marry anyone. You want to bring all the Real Love into your life that you can, and for that

reason—as I said in Chapter Four—you want to look for people who can be truthful, and who are interested in learning to be unconditionally loving.

But isn't it selfish, you might ask, to want to marry someone who is capable of unconditionally loving you? Sure, but your desire is healthy for *both* you and your prospective partner. We're here to experience all the love and happiness we can, and when it comes to choosing a lifelong partner, you want much more than just someone *you* can love. You need to find someone who can also add to *your* happiness. That is not a harmful desire, because you're not requiring that any single person change who they are, or that they suffer in any way. You're simply looking for someone with the characteristics that will make both of you happier.

Many people ask at this point, If I'm looking for someone capable of loving *me*, and I'll be trying to love *him* or *her*, isn't that a *trading* of love? Isn't that the definition of Imitation Love?

If your goal is to love someone *so that* he or she will love you in return, that *would* be conditional love, a form of Imitation Love. But that's not what you'll be doing when you understand Real Love. You'll be telling the truth about yourself and filling up with Real Love *before* you go looking for a spouse. Then you can give your partner the love you have without expectations that your love will be returned. If your partner already has sufficient Real Love, he or she will also give to you the love you need without expecting anything from you. When two people do this, they are mutually *sharing* love, not *trading* it. They are simultaneously offering a free gift, which is not dependent on what the other person offers. They each pour a river of love into an ocean which benefits both of them. They do not make their contribution to the relationship *if* their partner also makes one. They simply give what they have—freely—and then they enjoy the sum of their mutual giving.

> You can learn to love anyone, but when you're looking for a lifelong partner, you want to find someone who is also capable of unconditionally loving you. Then you'll enjoy a *sharing*—not a *trading*—of Real Love

The Criteria for Loving Someone Are Different from the Criteria for Marrying Someone

There is no greater joy than unconditionally accepting and loving other people, and you can learn to do that—in varying degrees—with everyone you know. But that doesn't mean you should be willing to *marry* any person you meet. Although you can find some measure of joy with anyone, you want to marry someone who can love you unconditionally and add significantly to your happiness.

When you say, "I love you because . . ." you are indicating that you want that person to continue being or doing something for your benefit. That is not compatible with Real Love, which means caring about the happiness of others without conditions. It is an entirely different matter, however, when you say, "I want to *marry* you because . . ." In that case, you're stating a belief that someone can *add* to your happiness, for a variety of reasons. You *should* choose a spouse based on his or her ability to add to the happiness of your relationship. When you properly pick a spouse, you first care about his or her happiness unconditionally—as you would do with anyone—and then you determine whether that person is also capable of receiving and returning that Real Love. We can learn to love anyone—unconditionally care about his or her happiness—but we need to be far more discriminating about who we choose to spend the rest of our lives with.

The difference between choosing people to love, and choosing someone to be a partner, is illustrated in the following story about Sylvia, who had been learning about Real Love for just a few months.

After dating Roger for two months, Sylvia called me to talk about him. "I like him," she said, "but it's pretty obvious he's received very little Real Love in his life."

Me: How can you tell that?

Sylvia: For one thing, he's angry a lot of the time. And he's pretty critical and blaming.

Me: So what's your question?

Sylvia: I don't know if I should keep dating him or not.

Me: What do you want most in your relationship?

Sylvia: Real Love, of course.

Me: From what you've seen so far, would Roger be bringing that to your relationship?

Sylvia: No, probably not, at least not right now. But maybe if I keep loving him, he'll feel more loved, and then he'll be able to love me, too.

Me: Have you ever climbed a mountain?

Sylvia: Yes, several times.

Me: If you had a choice, would you choose to climb a mountain *with* a hundred pound pack on your back, or *without* it?

Sylvia: Without it.

Me: Life is often like climbing a mountain. It can be difficult, strenuous, even frightening. You can choose to climb it with a hundred pounds on your back, or without.

Sylvia: You're talking about Roger.

Me: Yes. I am *not* telling you whether he's the right man for you. I am suggesting that because you're just learning about Real Love, the process of learning—feeling loved and loving others—could become much harder if you're carrying someone who doesn't know how to be honest or to love unconditionally.

Sylvia: I could teach him. If I leave him now, that wouldn't be loving on my part, would it?

Me: One of the reasons you're dating is to find a real partner, right? Someone to marry?

Sylvia: Yes.

Me: You can unconditionally love many people in your life, but you'll marry just one. Why make a decision to stay in a relationship with someone who is obviously handicapped—as far as Real Love is concerned—when it would be easier to learn about Real Love without that burden. Then, when you feel more loved and loving, you can find someone who is on the same path you are. Again, why climb the mountain with a hundred pound pack, when you could climb with no burden at all?

We love people unconditionally only because they need it, and because life is just more fulfilling when we're loving. When we're looking for a long-term partner, however, we need to raise the bar.

It's not healthy to look for someone to *make* us happy. We have that expectation only when we're empty and afraid, and in that condition, we will manipulate any partner we choose. We need to get as much Real Love as we can—to the point where our emptiness and fear are significantly diminished—and then look for someone who will *add* to the happiness we already have.

I suggest that the following criteria will prove most useful in finding a partner capable of an unconditionally loving relationship with you.

- The relative absence of Getting and Protecting Behaviors
- A minimum of addictions to Imitation Love
- An ability to tell the truth about his/her mistakes, flaws, and Getting and Protecting Behaviors.

The Relative Absence of Getting and Protecting Behaviors

Getting and Protecting Behaviors exist only in response to emptiness and fear, which are a result of insufficient Real Love. Since you want to minimize the emptiness and fear in your life, you want to choose a partner with as few Getting and Protecting Behaviors as possible. It's unrealistic to suppose that you'll find someone with *none* of these behaviors, but you can at least be aware of these behaviors as characteristics to avoid in a partner. We'll discuss variations on Getting and Protecting Behaviors in a following section, "How to Look for the Gold."

A Minimum of Addictions to Imitation Love

When people first use addictive drugs, they get a rush of satisfaction, or at least an escape from the pain of their lives. They soon discover that in order to get the same effect, they must use increasing quantities of their drug, and before long no amount will give them the relief they once experienced.

The use of Imitation Love is quite similar to the use of addictive drugs. At first, praise, power, pleasure, and safety feel pretty good in the absence of Real Love. But then we need more and more, and eventually no quantity of Imitation Love is satisfying.

In choosing a partner, we must look for the use of Imitation Love. If a partner has a strong compulsion to use sex, money, success in his/her career, conditional praise, and so on in order to feel good, that person will find it quite difficult to participate in a loving relationship with you. He or she will see you as just another source of Imitation Love, and when the positive effect you provide wears off, your relationship will disintegrate.

To be fair, anyone that doesn't have enough Real Love in his or her life—which describes almost all of us—will have some degree of dependency on Imitation Love. Don't look for someone who never uses Imitation Love, just someone who is less compulsive than most about his or her use of these Real Love substitutes. Even better, look for someone who can see and describe his or her own use of Imitation Love.

An Ability to Tell the Truth about His/Her Mistakes, Flaws, and Getting and Protecting Behaviors.

In Chapter Four, we discussed at length how to tell the truth about yourself. You want to find a partner who can do the same.

If you had to choose just one characteristic for determining whether a potential partner could participate in a loving relationship, it would be this: Can he or she easily admit being wrong. People who can admit their mistakes can learn anything. People who insist on being right are virtually incapable of learning—how can they learn something new when they already know everything?

> Can your partner easily admit being wrong? That
> might be the best single indication of whether he
> or she can participate in a loving relationship.

HOW TO LOOK FOR THE GOLD

In Chapter Four, I recommended that you not settle for anything
less than gold in relationships. Real Love is readily available
and infinitely superior to all of its substitutes. When you know
what the substitutes look like, you're much less likely to be
deceived by them. Following are just a few behaviors that will
help you sift the gold from the rocks. Keep in mind that we *all*
have flaws. You're not looking for perfection, just someone who
has the greatest possible yield.

An average gold mine produces roughly ten grams of gold
per ton of ore. That translates to one ounce of gold found in
about 100,000 ounces of rock. You can do a lot better than that
if you know what to look for.

- Does he call during the day for no reason other than to
  see how you're doing?

- Is it obvious that she's interested in every word you
  say?

- Does he light up whenever he sees you?

- Does she drop whatever she's doing to talk to you and
  spend time with you?

- Does he or she say, "I love you"?

We've all envisioned criteria like these, but I hasten to state
that they are not sufficiently reliable for choosing a partner. Why?
Early in relationships without enough Real Love, both partners
are eager to give one another as much Imitation Love as they

possibly can, for the purpose of maximizing the Imitation Love they receive in return—as we discussed in Chapter Two. Among the behaviors they exchange to win one another's approval are the "loving" behaviors listed above. Even in *conditionally* loving relationships, partners call one another frequently, send flowers, and so on. When we're "in love," we do a lot of things that appear to be loving. Without sufficient Real Love, however, the rewards fade, and when that happens, we're not willing to keep trying to win our partners' affection.

When we use loving behaviors for the purpose of winning affection from partners—in whatever form—that is not Real Love. No matter how good it feels, it's still just a trading of Imitation Love. The deception is usually mutual, and it's rarely conscious. It is deadly, however, to a relationship.

So, when someone fills the criteria above—calls, sends flowers, lights up on seeing you—how can you know whether it's Real Love or the initiation of an Imitation Love trade? One obvious answer is *time*. If you wait long enough, you'll find out whether someone is offering you Imitation Love, because it will always wear off. But that can take months, maybe longer, and by that time most people are engaged or married—at the very least they've invested a large portion of their lives in a very disappointing relationship.

Because positive behaviors are often unreliable indicators of Real Love, I suggest we look at the absence of negative characteristics as we look for a partner. When we're in love, it's pretty easy to pour on the positive behaviors, but it's much harder to hide the various forms of our Getting and Protecting Behaviors. We can learn a great deal about a potential partner, for example, as we look for the following:

• Irritation. He or she gets irritated pretty often at the common inconveniences of everyday life: heavy traffic, waiting in line, people who are late, and so on. Even though you might be wildly in love right now, his or her anger will eventually be directed at you, and because of the enormous expectations that come with exclusive relationships, that anger will focus on you more than on anyone else.

• Sex. Does he frequently make subtle—and not-so-subtle—references to sex? Does he stare at other women? Make comments about their bodies? Make excessive comments about *your* body? Does he lean on you to be more sexual with him than you're prepared to be? All these are indicators that he compulsively uses sex as a form of Imitation Love, and the likelihood is high that he'll use you as a "fix." More about sex in Chapter Seven.

• Sex. Does she sell sex as a way to attract men? Does she dress provocatively? Behave seductively? Such behavior can be exciting, but women often sell themselves as sexual objects precisely because they have little else to offer. When the excitement of the sex wears off—as it always does—what will you have?

• Bragging. Is he compelled to share with you every success and talent in his life? That need for conditional acceptance is crippling in a relationship.

• Controlling. When you're going out the door, she says, "Are you going to wear that?" If she can't let you choose your own clothes, imagine what she'll be choosing for you when you're married.

• Controlling. He gets irritated when you choose to go out with friends instead of spending time with him. If he tries to control you now—when you're just dating—imagine how he'll behave when you're married—when he believes he owns you.

• Power. Does he always have to win? At games, sports, arguments, whatever?

• Criticism. When you're driving, he/she is always making comments about your speed, the roads you choose, and so on. That may seem like an innocent thing, but that attitude will eventually spill over into everything else.

• Handshake. People with limp, weak handshakes usually carry those qualities over into other areas of their lives. With such a person, you'll likely be required to make all the major decisions in your relationship. He or she is also likely to act like a victim.

• Drinking. Even though the consumption of alcohol is widespread to the point of being normal, alcohol is simply a drug, and functions to depress our thinking and feeling. Do you want a relationship with someone who consistently uses alcohol as an escape from life?

• Complaining. Does your partner complain about the government, co-workers, bosses, parents, traffic, and so on? It's a guarantee that eventually the object of his or her complaints will be *you*.

• Eye contact. People who avoid eye contact are afraid, and they will deal with their fear by using the Protecting Behaviors that are so destructive in a relationship.

• Smiling. Is his or her smile relaxed and easy? Or is it strained and forced, designed to win your approval?

• Physical posture. When someone leans away from you, with arms and legs tightly crossed, that is a strong indication of fear and protecting.

• Punctuality. When she is consistently late, she's telling you that your time—and, by implication, *you*—is not important.

• Whining. People who claim to be victimized by people and circumstances *will* eventually be whining about you.

• Anger. Even though he may initially be directing his anger at others, his attacks will increasingly focus on you. Also keep in mind that anger easily turns into violence.

• Excuses. If she frequently makes excuses for her mistakes, you can count on her acting like a victim about many areas of her life.

• Clinging. He always wants to know where you are, and what you're doing, and he becomes anxious when you don't keep him informed. He's demanding your attention and affection, and that's a burden you don't want to take on yourself.

• Quiet. People who are shy or withdrawn are running. It may be cute in the beginning, but in the long run you'll feel like you're in the relationship all by yourself.

• Impatience. This is just another form of anger. If your partner gets impatient when he has to wait for you, you can be certain it will get much worse when your relationship becomes more committed.

• Listening. He gives no indication that he actually heard what you just said. Instead, he ignores you, or he leaps in to tell you something about himself. This is a strong indication that his concern is for himself, not for you.

• Secretive. He or she is protective about discussing past experiences and current activities.

• Talkative. He or she just can't allow a moment of uncomfortable silence when you're together. People who compulsively talk are trying to ensure that they are liked by others.

• Antsy. Just can't sit still. Has to be doing something all the time. Such people are trying to fill an emptiness that they often don't even recognize.

• Defensive. She quickly defends others if you say anything critical. It's very likely that she will similarly protect herself when she perceives any criticism.

• Driving. When people are impatient and dangerous as drivers, they're telling you about their relative disregard for the people around them.

CRITERIA TO AVOID:
WHAT NOT TO LOOK FOR

On many occasions I have asked men, "What are you looking for in a woman?" The answers are predictable:

- Attractive

- Nice breasts

- Sense of humor

- Similar interests (things in common, like sports, hiking, and so on)

- Wants children (or doesn't want children)

- Easy to talk to

- Intelligent

- Good family

- Responsible

The criteria women have for men are similar.

Be careful about the criteria you establish in your mind. On one occasion when I asked the question above, a man said, "She has to be pretty," and I responded, "If you're stuck on how she has to look, you might be missing the perfect woman for you."

What if the man or woman who would be a perfect partner for you happens to look a little different than you anticipated? Remember that most of us set standards for appearance and other outward characteristics based on our need for Imitation Love. Allow yourself to step free of your expectations, and instead look for the important qualities. When you find someone who is honest and loving, you'll be amazed at how little the other things matter.

You're looking for the best possible package, not just the most seductive wrapping.

Romance in Real Love

In Chapter Two, I said that falling in love is almost invariably nothing more than the relatively equal and abundant exchange of Imitation Love. In conjunction with that statement, I have often been asked, "So what is the role of romance in a Real Love relationship? Do you never get to fall in love with your partner?"

When people "fall" in love, they're not saying they fell into a sudden unconditional concern for another person's happiness. No, they're saying that another person gives every evidence of being able to fill a large portion of their emptiness with Imitation Love. That's exciting, but when the initial thrill wears off, the disappointment is huge. Infinitely more fulfilling is the following process:

- You tell the truth about yourself to many people, creating opportunities for them to see, accept, and love you.

- You exercise the faith necessary to accept and feel their love.

- Being filled with Real Love yourself, you begin to share that with others.

- You encounter someone who seems to have an unusually strong and appealing ability to be honest about himself/ herself, and has a strong desire to learn how to be unconditionally loving.

- In *addition* to the unconditional concern you feel for this person's happiness, you also experience the profound satisfaction that comes from feeling his or her love for you, his sense of humor, her talents, and so on.

- As you develop a relationship with someone who *adds* to the happiness you already have as a result of Real Love, that can be very exciting and romantic.

WHAT TO ASK, AND HOW TO EVALUATE IT

Your first introduction to a potential partner may be his or her profile on SoulMate.com. Those questions are designed to give people the opportunity to reveal who they really are. I also recognize, however, that someone could read Chapter Four and use it to create a falsely honest (interesting oxymoron) or deceptively loving image of himself or herself.

The answers people give to the Real Love essay questions are just a hint of who they are, to give you an idea of whether you want to pursue more contact by e-mail, phone, or in person. Let's review a few of those questions:

SoulMate.com Essay Questions

Describe a time you lied to a date, and why.

If someone can't think of a time when he or she has been less than honest, it's unlikely that you'll be having a honest discussion with that person about anything. Keep in mind, however, that lying is so common and accepted in our society that people often need help seeing their lies.

When you meet with a partner in person, you can ask for more examples of lying. Remember that when you ask someone for examples of their lying, you're only creating opportunities to see and accept one another. You're not staging an inquisition.

You agree to meet your date at a restaurant at 7:30 p.m., but at the appointed time, he/she is not there. How long would you wait? At the end of the time you wait, as you're walking to your car, you run into your date on his/her way to the restaurant. What would you say to him/her about being late?

Is he concerned only about his own inconvenience, or does he show some sign of understanding and compassion? This is also a great opportunity for you to talk about the times you have been late and selfish.

How did your last two relationships end? How was any of that your fault?

If your date goes on and on about the faults of her ex-partner, that's a great predictor of how she'll be talking about your faults before long. In Chapter Four you'll find examples of truthfully answering this question.

On average, you have sex with a partner after how many dates? If your partner isn't interested in sex after that many dates, what do you usually do?

You'll see the real answer to this question more in your partner's behavior than in his or her words. He may *say* he can wait to have sex, but if he leans on you to be more and more sexual with him, you'll learn the truth about his attitude.

Describe something (or someone) that irritates you. Now describe what that irritation says about you.

This is a difficult question for people to answer if they haven't read the *Real Love* book. Until we have the language for Real Love and Getting and Protecting Behaviors, it's hard to make sense of our anger.

While on a date, you notice that your partner keeps looking at other men/women as they walk by. What would you say?

What matters here is not so much *what* your partner says here, but whether it's expressed with irritation.

What do you fear most when you go out on a date?

Everybody has fears on a date, and I listed a number of them in Chapter Four. A partner who can express them openly will be much more likely to participate in an honest and loving relationship.

Describe a moment in your life that still brings you pain as you think of it.

Can your partner talk about his or her stupid mistakes and embarrassing moments? That's a very positive sign.

Describe a mistake you made recently at work.

Again, you're looking for candor. The details aren't important.

Asking Questions Live (Phone and in Person)

After you've read someone's profile, and you've determined that you want to know more about this person, you'll want to meet with him or her in person, or by phone. We'll talk more about how to do that in the next chapter. Some people can fake honesty in a written profile, but in real time, they *will* reveal who they are, especially if you ask the kind of questions suggested below. When you understand Real Love, and Getting and Protecting Behaviors, you'll see that people reveal who they are with every breath they take. Most people will be more specific and revealing in person than they are in filling out an online form.

You might ask:

- "In your SoulMate profile, you mentioned a couple of things that irritate you. What are some other things that bother you?"

- "What do you wish you could change about your job?" Look for a tendency on the part of your partner to act like a victim, blaming other people for how he or she feels.

- "I noticed that you didn't answer all the SoulMate essay questions. Why is that?" A partner reluctant to tell the truth is unlikely to be able to function in a loving relationship.

- "Tell me about some really bad dates you've had." Watch for the tendency to blame other people.

- "Have you read the *Real Love* book. Is that something you'd be willing to do?"

- "Where do your parents live? Do you see them often?" Many years ago I heard someone say to a group of teenage girls, "Watch for how your date treats his mother. It's a strong predictor for how he'll treat you." There's a lot of truth to that. If your date has withdrawn from his parents, blaming them for the separation, he will likely do the same thing to you when you offend him.

- Ask him a question that gives him an opportunity to brag about himself.

To learn more about relationships, and the qualities to look for in a partner, read the book, *Real Love—The Truth About Finding Unconditional Love and Fulfilling Relationships* (Go to http://www.gregbaer.com/book/book.asp).

℘ *Chapter Six* ℃

Bumping Up the Yield

The Techniques of Dating

Great dating is not a technique. It's a natural result of two people who are willing to be honest and accepting. As you're learning to be open and loving, however, there are some details about dating that will help you make the experience as rewarding as possible.

WHEN TO DATE

Although we briefly discussed in Chapter Four the need to have some measure of Real Love before we date, this subject is so important that we'll talk more about it here. Productive dating requires honesty and the presence of Real Love. With that in mind, don't begin to date:

- When you feel empty and afraid. In that condition, you *will* manipulate your partner for Imitation Love, and you'll protect yourself, making a loving relationship impossible

- Too soon after the failure of a relationship. Right after a break-up, you'll be so needy that you won't be able to avoid clinging, manipulating, and so on. Especially in the case of a divorce, wait long enough that you can date without any hint of desperation. I usually recommend that people wait a year after a divorce before they begin dating.

- When you're in the middle of a crisis: You lost your job, your dog died, your house was swept away by a hurricane.

- When you're physically not well. Women, for example, should never date during a time when the likelihood is high that they'll be suffering from premenstrual syndrome (PMS).

What if you're already dating? If you don't already have enough Real Love from friends and family—enough that you are largely free of emptiness and fear—it's virtually a certainty that you're having considerable difficulties in your present relationship. In that case, it's usually wise to break off that relationship and get the Real Love you need to be healthy and happy. Once you feel unconditionally loved, you'll have the tools to date in a healthy way. Shortly we'll discuss an example of someone who learned this principle. Chapter Nine provides a more detailed discussion of what to do with an already difficult relationship.

Let me suggest that you ask yourself the following questions to help you determine whether you're ready to date:

- Do I feel lonely?

- Do I worry about not having enough dates?

- Do I worry about what my partner will think of me?

- Do I feel like I *need* a man? Or need a woman?

- Am I looking for somebody to make me happy?

- Will I be crushed if my date doesn't want to ask me out again?

- Do I worry about how I look and what I'll say when I'm on a date?

- Are you heartbroken about a recently lost relationship?

If your answer to these questions is *yes*, your emptiness and fear will cause you to seek Imitation Love, and will significantly distract you from the kind of relationship you really need.

How To Prepare To Look For a Partner

Before you're capable of finding a healthy intimate or exclusive relationship, you must eliminate your emptiness and fear—not completely, but to a large extent—with Real Love. You can get that love from *anyone* who has it, as Sandra learned here from her discussion with me.

Sandra: I've been dating William for several months, and it just doesn't seem to be working out. We're always arguing, and I don't know what to do.

Me: You don't have nearly enough Real Love in your life to participate in a loving relationship, and that's what you really want, isn't it?

Sandra: Sure, but what can I do about that?

I described the process of finding Real Love, and suggested that she start telling the truth about herself to some girlfriends and family members.

Sandra: But what about William?

Me: I can't tell you what you should do with a particular partner, but I *can* tell you the pattern I've observed with hundreds of other couples. Right now you need to feel more Real Love in your life, something you've been missing for a long time. It's the most important goal you could pursue, and you need to avoid anything that might get in your way. With your own experience, you've already proven that it's very unlikely you could have a genuinely loving relationship with William. You're not ready to be unconditionally loving, and neither is he. If you stay in a relationship with him now—while you're empty and afraid—you will not be able to avoid having huge expectations of him, and those expectations will seriously distract you from your goal of feeling Real Love. You'll be too disappointed and irritated when he doesn't give you what you need."

If you're not married, and you don't have enough Real Love to participate in a mutually loving relationship, finding Real Love is the most important effort you can make, *not* finding or preserving a relationship with any particular partner. It's usually not productive to keep trying to repair a relationship—other than marriage—that's not unconditionally loving. Instead, recognize that you're not ready for a dating relationship, and then learn how to find the Real Love you need from friends. When there is insufficient love in a relationship—other than marriage—it's usually wise to break off that relationship and get the Real Love you need. We'll talk in Chapter Nine about how to end relationships that aren't working.

> Do not date until you have enough Real Love in your life that you have largely eliminated your emptiness and fear. Otherwise, you will be desperate for Imitation Love, and will ruin every relationship you begin.

Don't Date Until You're Really Ready

The solution to Sandra's situation is not for her to leave William and then immediately fill his place with another man. She needs to get sufficient Real Love from other *women* and from men for whom she feels no sexual attraction. She probably won't be prepared to date in a healthy way for many months, or longer. If she starts looking for an exclusive relationship before she is sufficiently whole and loving, she *will* have another unhappy experience.

When we leave a relationship that's not working, we tend to dull our pain by replacing it with yet another relationship that won't work. We'd rather have *some* attention—even if it's not based on Real Love—than no attention at all. All our lives, most of us have been using other people for the Imitation Love they give us, much as we'd use an addictive drug. When we break up with a partner, we often experience the terrible discomfort of withdrawal. To eliminate that pain, we go back to using our drug—the praise, power, and pleasure we get from other people—and then we're stuck in a cycle that never ends.

The best way out of this addictive trap is to step completely out of the cycle. We have to make conscious decisions to avoid using people for the Imitation Love they give us, even when we feel empty and alone and desperately need a "fix." If you feel like you really *need* a woman (or man) in your life, you're not ready to date.

HOW CAN YOU MEET MEN?
HOW CAN YOU MEET WOMEN?

There are many places you can meet other singles:

- School
- Work
- Church groups. Most churches now have singles groups.
- Professional matchmakers
- Special interest groups or clubs (Greenpeace, bird watchers, book clubs)

- Service organizations

- Singles cruises

- Athletic leagues (softball, volleyball, tennis)

- Adult education classes

- The Internet (SoulMate.com)

- Supermarket

- Twelve-step meetings

- Through friends

- Charity fund raisers

- Bookstores

- Dance groups/clubs/classes

Each of these has its pluses and minuses. I'd like to spend some time discussing the advantages of Internet dating.

Dating on the Internet

A hundred years ago, it's likely that you would have lived your entire life in the same town. You would have worked near your home, and you would have known everyone in the neighborhood or town. When you asked someone out, you would already have known a great deal about him or her.

Times have changed. Now we're not likely to work near the place where we were raised. We don't know our neighbors well, and we tend to have numerous superficial relationships. Almost everyone is a stranger, and in that environment you're trying to figure out who you should date.

Let's examine the odds of a heterosexual woman finding a suitable partner in random situations. Assume that she's surveying a room of 100 random people. Half are men (leaving a pool of 50 still eligible). Of the half who are men, half are married (now 25 left). Of those, only 6 are remotely within the right age range for you. One of those is gay (5 remaining). Two are seriously dating someone else (3). Two are absolutely unsuitable for reasons of religion, politics, or financial stability. From the original pool of 100 people, only one person is a serious possibility for a date, and this scenario isn't exaggerated in the least.

Those are pretty lousy odds, and this is just for finding a man eligible on the basis of age, religion, and some of the basics. If, in addition, she wants to find a man capable of engaging in an unconditionally loving relationship, she'd have to survey a great number of rooms filled with a hundred people. That would be very costly in terms of time, energy, money, travel—as most daters can attest.

On SoulMate.com, you can find a partner with a great deal more efficiency. You type into the search engine your requirements for age, location, race, and other characteristics that matter to you, and in a heartbeat you're given twenty men— perhaps more, perhaps less—who are real possibilities. With the additional use of the Real Love essay questions, in minutes you can narrow the field even further to those who are interested in a relationship based on unconditional love.

> Internet dating is simply the most efficient way to meet people and make the initial selection of potential partners.

Internet dating is the most efficient way available to quickly find a pool of men or women that meet your requirements for a relationship. How does Internet dating work? Follow these easy steps:

- Create a profile
- Post a photo of yourself

- Use the search engine to define qualities in a partner that are important to you (age, location, and so on)

- Read the profiles—multiple choice and yes/no questions—of Members selected by your search requirements

- Read the Real Love essay questions of the men/women whose multiple-choice profiles interest you

- E-mail those you'd like to learn more about

- Conduct an e-mail relationship until you're comfortable with moving to the next level

- Exchange phone numbers with your partner

- Conduct a phone relationship until you're comfortable with moving to the next level

- Meet in person

Create a Profile

We discussed this subject in Chapter Four. Be honest about who you are. If you lie, your relationship is immediately founded on a deception, and you will not like the eventual result. *Always* fill out the Real Love essay questions, since those will best communicate who you are to other Members.

As you answer the essay questions, don't talk to much. That often seems pushy and desperate. Have a friend check your grammar, so you don't come across as more illiterate than you really are. Don't talk too much about sex, unless you want that to be the foundation of your relationship.

Post a Photo of Yourself

Many people refuse to post a photo, claiming that it doesn't really represent who they are. They protest that they don't want to cater to the superficial judgments of people who make decisions based on appearance.

I understand that objection, and I agree with it, but it's a simple fact that people who post their photos get *ten* times more e-mail contacts than those who don't post a photo. Remember that your photo isn't your entire profile. You're also answering the Real Love essay questions, which will reveal who you are.

Some suggestions about photos:

- People will get to know you better if you post a couple of photos, in different settings and with different moods.

- The goal is portray yourself as you really are, not to paint a false picture. Pick a photo where you're relaxed, rather than one that portrays you in a falsely glamorous way.

- Women, do not emphasize your sexual characteristics. I know that's very tempting—since we're taught almost everywhere we go that it's sex that sells—but don't do it. Many women post a picture of themselves in a bikini, or low-cut dress, and then they wonder why men are interested in them only for sex. Hardly a surprise. Most women have no idea how sexually fixated men can be. If you post a photograph that includes your torso, most men will notice your breasts first—even if you're fully clothed. Do you really want to be treated like a pair of breasts?

- Men, don't emphasize your body. Don't wear a tank top to emphasize your muscles. You'll be painting a picture of yourself that will not tend to attract people interested in Real Love.

- You should be the only living thing in the photo. Don't use a photo of you with a child or a pet.

- Don't wear too much make-up or jewelry.

- Relaxed smile. If you look pained or strained, you'll scare most people off.

- Pick a photo that friends have said is flattering of you.

Define Qualities You're Looking for

This is where you define the general qualities you require in a partner: age, location, religion, and so on. Be careful about being too picky here, or you might rule out someone who is perfect for you, but was just outside the parameters you set.

Read the Profiles of Other Members

Remember that you're not looking for someone who is perfect. You're looking for someone headed in the same *direction* you are—someone who is diligently working at being honest and unconditionally loving, and who is making consistent progress toward those goals.

E-mail Those You'd like to Learn More about

E-mail the first ten or twelve contacts that interest you. Don't settle for just one, and don't be hurt if you don't get a response from most of them. Many of the people you contact will already have found a partner, or they're no longer available for other reasons and just haven't removed their profiles.

Many people—especially women—don't send out e-mails. They wait for others to contact them. Not smart. The idea of Internet dating is to sift through people as quickly as possible, and you'll do that best if you proactively contact as many people as you can.

What should you say in that first e-mail? Keep it simple, something like this: "I read your profile on SoulMate.com, and I'd like to get to know more about you. If you're interested, please respond."

On some e-mail services, the system automatically puts your name in the return e-mail address. For example, you might write heavenlybabe@coolserver.com, but in the message coolserver. com might indicate that it's from <SylviaSmith>heavenlybabe

@coolserver.com. You can determine what your server does by sending out sample e-mails to some friends, who will tell you what the return addresses states. If your server includes your name, and you don't want people to know your name in the beginning of your contacts with them, you can contact your server and ask how to eliminate your name from the return address.

Conduct an E-mail Relationship

Most of us don't communicate well in writing—our language becomes stiff and formal. As you write, try to be as relaxed as possible, expressing yourself as you would speak in person.

It should be noted that sometimes we're a great deal more bold in writing than we are in person, and that can lead to inappropriately intimate revelations. You might want to restrain yourself from sharing the most intimate details by e-mail. Those are better communicated in person.

By e-mail you can ask most of the questions recommended for face-to-face dates, which we discussed in Chapter Five. Beware of offering critical comments by e-mail. When people read something about themselves, they tend to hear it in the voice of the most disapproving person they've ever known. As much as 93% of our communication is non-verbal, so when we communicate by e-mail—lacking the non-verbal component—the potential for miscommunication is huge.

Keep a file for each person you're e-mailing. This will keep you from getting confused about any one person you're writing to. It will keep you from mistakenly asking, for example, "So how's your mother?" when she told you two days ago that her mother died.

Exchange Phone Numbers with Your Partner

How long should you communicate by e-mail before you exchange phone numbers? As long as it takes until you're comfortable that you know your partner fairly well. If you and your partner are open and honest, you can move through the e-mail stage of your relationship in a matter of days. Phone conversations are a great deal more revealing and rewarding than e-mails. On the phone you can hear inflections, tone of voice, and many other subtleties that are expressed vocally. You can also see how your partner answers on the spur of the moment, without time to think about it.

You need to understand that once you've given out your home phone number, you've essentially given out your address, since there are many ways that people can find your address once they know your phone number. For that reason, you don't want to give out your home phone until you're comfortable that you know your partner fairly well.

If you want to make phone contact before you're willing to give out your address, you can use a cell phone, a pay phone, or a pre-paid calling card to make your calls. With those tools, your location can remain unknown.

Conduct a Phone Relationship

If you're any judge of character at all, you should be able to move past the phone stage of your relationship within days or weeks.

Meet in Person

The first time you meet your date in person, remember that at this point you probably don't know him or her well. For that reason, you might consider taking reasonable precautions:

- Tell at least one friend where you'll be meeting your date, and roughly what time you'll call your friend when the date is finished.

- Carry a cell phone with you.

- Meet your date at the location where you'll be doing something together, rather than having your date pick you up.

- Meet in a public place. You probably wouldn't want your first date to be in the northern Canadian woods, a cave, or an abandoned oil refinery.

- Don't leave your drink on the table when you're not there to watch it. Although the incidence of people using the "date rape" drug is low, it's a possibility you need to be aware of.

Although you want to ensure your safety as much as possible, you want to do that with wisdom and caution, not with paranoia and an air of protection. If you're frightened, you'll ruin your interactions with anyone.

Later in the chapter, I'll describe many activities that have proven highly successful for a first or second date.

ASKING

Few things provoke more anxiety than asking someone for a date the first time. Men who have been heroes in combat turn into trembling children when faced with asking a woman if she'll go out with them. On many occasions—years ago—I dialed the first six digits of a woman's phone number, only to hang up before I finished dialing the whole number. My experience was not unique.

When you ask someone for a date, you're really putting yourself out there. You're exposing yourself to rejection in a big way. Asking for a date is like a combination of public speaking, applying for a job, and performing in an audition, all rolled into one. Yikes!

Eliminating the Anxiety of Asking

How can you eliminate the anxiety of asking for a date? How can you eliminate the anxiety of dating itself? The two-part answer is the same for both questions: First, a new intellectual understanding; and second, filling your own emptiness.

Change the Way You See Dating

In Chapter Four I proposed a new way of looking at dating. Your goal in dating is not to *get* anyone to like you. Rather, your goal is to *find out* who is capable of loving you. With the latter goal in mind, you realize that when someone rejects you early in a relationship—even at the first phone call—they're doing you a *favor*. The faster you can see that a particular relationship is impossible, the sooner you can move on to developing other relationships.

Fill Your Emptiness

Our greatest fear is that we won't be loved, that we'll remain empty and alone. Our fears in dating are the same. We're concerned about not receiving two dollars from a specific person, forgetting that the real goal for all of us is to find twenty million dollars—Chapter Three—wherever we can get it. As you take the steps of finding Real Love from as many friends as family members as possible, you'll feel like you have twenty million dollars, and then it will no longer matter to you whether a particular person gives you two dollars.

Every time you're upset or anxious, you're claiming that the only love in the universe is the piece that's being withheld from you in that moment. When you get enough Real Love in your life, you can see that the supply is infinite, and then you don't have to get any one person's affection.

Who Should Do the Asking?

In many cultures, men have for centuries assumed the responsibility for asking women for their time, attention, and commitment. Times are changing, however, and it is now far more acceptable for women to do the asking. In a recent survey of thousands of men and women, half the men said that they would like to eliminate the custom of men carrying the sole responsibility for asking women out on a date. Half the women indicated that they were tired of having to sit back and wait for men to call them.

> If you want to meet as many people as possible, you must be willing to do the asking.

More and more, men and women prefer that either sex feel free to make the initial call. If women sit around waiting for men to initiate relationships, they will often miss out on some great opportunities, as my friend Connie discovered. She called me one day to let me know how her life was going.

Connie: As you know, I take a night class in accounting.

Me: How's that going?

Connie: Class is fine, but more important, there's a man in the class I really like. We've spoken several times, and I wish he'd ask me out.

Me: Why should it be *his* job to ask *you* out? Why can't you ask him?

Connie: I guess I could, but the thought of asking him makes me pretty nervous.

Me: And you think *he's* not nervous when he asks women out? Why should you dump the job of asking on him?

Connie: I guess I'm still relying a bit on that old tradition that the guys do the asking.

Me: And look what you're getting by playing that old
           game. All these months, you could have been
           developing a relationship with him, but you've been
           too afraid to ask.

Connie did ask him out, and she had a wonderful time with
him.

In dating you begin to establish the pattern of your
relationship. If you eventually expect to be equal partners with
your future spouse, why would you abdicate now your right
to participate equally in the initial asking? Will you require
him to make the first move in everything else throughout your
relationship? People who wait for others to make a move are
often being fearful and irresponsible. They wait for others to
take the risks, and then they're critical later of the choices made.
Not a great way to run a relationship.

If you want to get to know someone better, take the
responsibility for creating time together. That takes courage, but
the reward is well worth the risks.

Ladies, on occasion you will run into a man who is offended
that you would ask him for a date. He believes that upsets the
natural order of things. He's just telling you that he's unfamiliar
with that pattern of behavior, and afraid that he might lose control.
If he's offended over this, imagine how many other things will
offend him in a relationship.

How to Ask

If you've met someone on SoulMate.com, and you've established
an e-mail and phone relationship with that person, asking him or
her out on a date is pretty easy: "I've enjoyed getting to know
you by e-mail and on the phone. I'd like to meet you in person.
Would you be interested in that?"

If you meet someone outside an Internet setting, asking is still simple:

- "Would you like to go out sometime?"

- "I've enjoyed meeting you. Would you like to go out sometime?"

- "I'd like to spend more time with you—get to know you. Would you be interested in that?"

- "I've enjoyed the time we've spent together. Could I have your number (or your e-mail address)?"

- "I'd love to call you. Could I have your number? If you're not comfortable with that, I could just give you mine." Now she'll feel safer, and she can offer her number if she wishes.

With these questions, you'll learn in seconds whether that person has any interest in dating you. If they're hesitant, or make excuses, or say *no*, you're free to move on.

When the Answer is "Yes"

If the answer to your request for a date is *yes*, now you can work out the details. If you're the one asking, it's your responsibility to propose an activity for the date: lunch, a sporting event, taking a walk. These are just initial ideas. If you see hesitation from your partner about your first or second suggestion, ask him/her what she would like to do instead. Keep talking until you're both delighted with the plan. Following are samples of how you might work out a date:

- "I don't really enjoy fishing, but I'd like to do something else with you. How about riding bicycles?"

- "Tuesday won't work, but Thursday evening would be good."

- "Everybody has different preferences, so I won't assume I know yours. I usually pick my date up, but what would you like?"

- "I usually pay for the date. Is that all right with you?"

- "I like to pay my own way on a first date—then I don't feel obligated in any way. Is that all right with you?"

We'll discuss dating activities later in this chapter.

When the Answer Is "Maybe"

Sometimes you'll ask for a date, and the response is equivocal, hesitant, reluctant. Do *not* pressure that person for an acceptance. Remember your goal to get to "no" faster, and make it as easy as possible for the other person to refuse you gracefully. You might say, "Hey, you appear uncertain about this. If so, just say so, because I'm not trying to get you to do anything. You will not hurt my feelings. Really."

Saying "No" to a Request for a Date

If you're asked on a date, and you're not interested in spending time with that person, do *not* play around. Don't make excuses, or lead him/her on. One reason we're reluctant to say *no* is that we're afraid of hurting the other person's feelings. If you say *no* right from the beginning, your rejection probably will sting a bit, but the alternative is much worse. If you communicate various forms of *maybe*—but you mean *no*—it's a cruel trick you're playing. You leave the other person twisting in the wind, burdened with the task of figuring out what you really mean. Tell the truth and let him or her go.

Most of the time, when we claim to be trying not to hurt someone else's feelings, we're really avoiding our own discomfort—the pain of that person not liking us as a result of something we said or did.

When you want to refuse a request for a date, say *no* directly and gracefully:

- "No, but thanks for asking."
- "No, I wouldn't, but it was flattering of you to ask."

What if someone asks you out, or asks for your phone number, and you're just not sure about what you want to do at that point? Ask for his or her phone number, and then it's up to you whether you will make further contacts.

WHAT TO DO ON A FIRST OR SECOND DATE

Your dates will be far more productive if you plan an activity designed to help you fulfill the two primary purposes of dating:

- To practice sharing who you are with other
- To find people who are capable of being truthful, and who have a sincere interest in learning to love unconditionally

Sure, you also want to have fun on a date, but primarily you want to create opportunities to know one another. I suggest the following guidelines in planning a first or second date (in addition to the two above):

- Keep the cost down. If you feel a need to make the date expensive, it's likely you're trying to impress your partner. Moreover, you'll be setting a standard you might not be prepared to keep up.
- Keep it short. Don't make your first date a long evening, or a weekend. If you discover you don't like one another in the first five minutes, you'll have a real problem.
- Keep it public. If your date doesn't already know you well, he or she will feel safer meeting with you in a place where there are many other people.

- Keep it casual. Avoid situations where either of you could feel pressured to be prematurely intimate. Don't say, "Let's go back to my place," and don't accept such an offer.

Following are a few activities that would not be appropriate for a first date, according to the guidelines above:

- An evening alone, for any reason (dinner in your apartment, a quiet chat by your fireplace)

- A long trip together. Too much time, expense, and intimacy.

- Swimming or other activity that usually involves wearing skimpy clothing. Too intimate.

- Drinking alcohol in any form. How can you show someone who you really are when your mind is being altered by a drug?

- Anything where you're competing with your partner. Competition doesn't usually foster expressing who we are, or feeling accepted. Engaging in an athletic activity—table tennis, basketball—is fine as long as you don't keep score. If your partner is expressing frustration at his or her performance in an athletic activity, stop and do something else.

- A formal dance

- Dinner with your family. Way too much pressure to perform.

- Sex. It creates an enormous sense of false intimacy. We'll address this subject in detail in Chapter Seven.

- Movies are often not the best activities for a first date, because mostly you're not talking to one another.

- Gambling. It just doesn't have the right atmosphere for an honest sharing of who you are.

> Simple guidelines for a first or second date:
>
> •Keep the cost down.
>
> •Keep it short.
>
> •Keep it public.
>
> •Keep it casual.

Following are just a few activities that do fulfill the above guidelines:

- Lunch. Easily my personal favorite. It has a nicely defined beginning and end (no should-I-invite-him-in discomfort at the end), and it's inexpensive and public. Nine out of ten daters have said that on a first date they would prefer lunch or a drink after work.
- A walk in a residential area of town.
- Meeting for coffee after work.
- A sporting event in the daytime
- Picnic in a public park
- Going to a museum
- Doing some volunteer project together
- Walk around the mall.

Double Dating

What about double dating, or group dating? There are advantages and disadvantages to this kind of dating, and you'll have to consider these as you make your own decision.

Advantages of double or group dating:

- Eliminates much of the pressure of premature intimacy. Many people feel less pressure on a date when they're with several people, not just one.

- You can observe how your date interacts with other people.

- If you go out with another couple you know well— people from whom you feel unconditional acceptance— that Real Love may help you behave more naturally with your date.

Disadvantages of double or group dating:

- On a double date, some people tend to interact more with the couple they already know, leaving the date feeling like the odd man (or woman) out.

- You date might feel an additional pressure to please multiple people, not just you, and then he or she would behave unnaturally.

- Your date may be more reluctant to share personal details in a crowd.

WHAT TO TALK ABOUT

In Chapter Four I proposed many ways to tell the truth about ourselves. Use them. I'm not saying your entire date should be about truth telling, but don't be satisfied with only superficial banter. Life's too short to be satisfied with fluff.

There are so many ways to initiate meaningful conversations:

- Tell me about something you did today that you really enjoyed.

- Tell me about an experience you had today that was really annoying.

- Tell me more about your job. What do you like most about it? Least?

- Today in the newspaper I read that _____. I feel _____ about that. How about you?

- In your SoulMate.com profile, you said _____. Would you be willing to talk more about that?

- I've been reading _____ (book). Is there a particular kind of book you enjoy reading?

- Last week I saw _____ (movie). Did you see it? What did you think of it?

- My parents live in _____. I see them a couple of times a year, but I call them every week or two. Tell me about your family.

- Do you have pets? Tell me about them.

If there is any confusion about what your date says—the kind of thing where later you wish you'd known what he meant—*ask*. Confusion is a terrible obstacle to loving relationships.

Be very slow indeed to say, "I love you." Enormous commitment is implied with that statement, and you want to be pretty sure before you speak those words.

Don't be too quick to comment about your partner's physical appearance. If you say to her, "You are so beautiful," even though she might enjoy the flattery, she also hears that she has to *stay* beautiful in order for you to continue liking her. There's also a large element of selfishness in telling a woman she's beautiful, because what you're really saying is that she gives *you* the physical pleasures of looking at her and fantasizing about her. Telling her that she's beautiful is more about you than her.

The most important thing you could do when your partner is speaking is to listen—genuinely listen. Most of us don't know how to do that. While we're empty and afraid, we can only look at conversations as opportunities to get more attention for ourselves, and to protect ourselves. You can learn a great deal

more about how to listen, and how to use the Rules of Seeing, in
*Real Love—The Truth About Finding Unconditional Love and
Fulfilling Relationships*, and in *The Wise Man—The Truth About
Sharing Real Love.*

Truth telling Later in the Relationship

You don't want to share everything about yourself on the first
couple of dates. That would be too much for almost anyone to
hear. Stick with the kinds of things we talked about in Chapter
Four. After you've dated several times, though, you need to be
talking about some of your more serious mistakes and flaws.
Why is that necessary? We'll see the answer to that as we watch
my interaction with Jennifer.

Jennifer: I've dated Eric five times in the last month, and I
             really like him, but now I'm wondering how much I
             should tell him about myself.

Me: What are you afraid to tell him?

Jennifer: Years ago, when I was even more stupid than I am
             now—I was just a kid—I got pregnant and had an
             abortion. I'm wondering if I should tell him about
             that. Nobody knows.

Me: The answer depends on where you see your
             relationship going with this guy. The first question is
             whether you're ready to get married.

Jennifer: Yes, I'm interested in getting married. I'm not sure
             yet whether Eric is the right one.

Me: Once you think Eric is even a serious possibility—
             and that doesn't have to be right now—you need to
             tell him everything about you.

Jennifer: Why? Why can't we just leave it alone? Nobody knows, and nobody has to know.

Me: If you don't tell the truth about the abortion to the person you think might become your spouse—and tell the truth about anything else you've been keeping a secret—you'll always live with some measure of fear. You'll wonder, What if he finds out somehow? What if he couldn't love me after finding out? For your own peace, you'd need to tell your prospective spouse.

Jennifer: Could I wait until after we're married?

Me: What if the thing you're afraid to tell him is the one thing he just couldn't live with? If you wait until right before the wedding—or, much worse, after the wedding—you'll have wasted all that time, and invested all that emotional energy, for nothing.

If you're really being honest about yourself, you should know after two or three dates whether the person your dating is a possibility for a long-term committed relationship. I realize that telling the truth about intimate things is somewhat risky, but the reward—feeling more unconditionally loved—is enormous. Only you can know the timing for sharing.

The Book, *Real Love—The Truth About Finding Unconditional Love and Fulfilling Relationships*

One of the most powerful tools you can use to initiate truth telling on a date is also one of the easiest to implement. I received the following letter from a woman in Texas:

When I first read the *Real Love* book over a year ago, I knew I'd found the answer to my own happiness, and to finding a loving partner. I've had a lot of lousy relationships in the past, and I made a decision I wasn't going to do that anymore. So I started telling the truth about myself on dates, just a little at a time, nothing heavy. But then I added one more thing to every first date, and that has made a huge difference. At the end of every first date—if he was interested in a second date—I've said to the guy I was with, "I've been reading a book that has taught me more about relationships than anything I've ever come across. Would you be willing to read it?"

Then I tell them about the *Real Love* book. If he's not interested in reading about the principles that create great relationships, I quit dating him. Why date somebody who isn't interested in the most important thing in the world, right? But I found a handful of men who were fascinated by the subject, and now I'm engaged to one of them.

The *Real Love* book is a great way to weed out the partners who aren't interested in the kind of relationship you want.

THE DETAILS OF DATING

Even though great dating is a natural product of telling the truth about yourself and learning how to love unconditionally, it's also helpful to discuss some of the details about dating that will influence the process of finding the person you want.

Physical Appearance: Clothes, Make-up, Hair

Look natural. If you put too much effort into your appearance, you'll be deceiving your partner.

Dress modestly. I had a friend once who took a particular delight in pointing out the hypocrisy of others (keep in mind as you read the following story that I do not condone or recommend his approach). On one occasion we were in an airport together, and he noticed a woman sitting not far away who was wearing a low-cut dress. He walked over, sat down opposite her, and stared intently at her breasts. After a few moments, the woman said, "What are you staring at?"

"Your breasts, of course," said my friend.

The woman gasped and said, "How dare you!"

"How dare I?" said my friend. "You intentionally chose a dress that would attract men to your breasts, and now I'm just fulfilling your wish. I don't see the problem here."

With every choice we make, we declare who we are, and what we want. If you dress like a prostitute, what kind of men do you think you'll attract? Think about how you want to be seen, and what kind of people that will bring into your life.

Be clean and neat. This should be obvious to everyone, but there really are people who don't quite understand this point. Never go on a date without showering, brushing you teeth, and at least making sure that straw isn't hanging from your hair. Carry breath mints, breath spray, or chewing gum with you at all times (I'm not kidding here). Poor hygiene is the ultimate turn-off on a date.

Compliments

We all love to hear compliments, and therein is a huge potential trap. If you *need* to hear compliments, you're using praise as a form of Imitation Love. If your partner requires compliments, be aware that you'll never fill up that person's emptiness.

It is possible, however, to give and receive healthy praise. Stay aware from superficial compliments, especially those having to do with physical appearance. Instead offer positive statements about your partner's choices. When he or she is honest about a mistake or failing, for example, you could say, "Beautiful. I admire your honesty." Other examples of healthy compliments:

- "You've really worked hard to succeed in your career. That must feel good."

- "Not many people talk about their own responsibility for being angry. I appreciate your sharing that with me."

- "What he said to you was pretty hateful. I admire the way you handled your response."

- "It's refreshing to hear someone take responsibility for a failed relationship. I admire that."

- "You seem very relaxed and natural. It's pleasantly disarming."

- "This whole evening, I haven't felt like you're trying to impress me, and I love that. It sure is easier to get to know someone who isn't trying to shove their resume down my throat."

- "Most people are afraid of silence in a conversation. Makes them uneasy. But you're not. That takes real confidence."

Silence

Most of us are uncomfortable with silence. When there is no conversation, we worry about what our partner will think of us. We worry that we'll be seen as inarticulate. If you have nothing to say, say nothing. That takes a measure of confidence.

Punctuality

Be on time. When you're late, you're declaring that your time is more important than everyone else's, and that's not a great way to start a relationship. If you are late, don't make excuses. Honestly describe how you made some poor choices.

What if your date is late? It is not your job to correct every wrong in the universe. You're not the punctuality proctor. When your date is late, simply file that as a piece of information that will help you determine whether you want to pursue the relationship further.

WHO TO DATE

Occasionally, reach outside your usual parameters of location, age, height, and weight, and see what you learn. Be open. If you learn only that you can't live with those variations, it will still be a valuable lesson.

It's a huge mistake to look only for someone who has a lot in common with you. For one thing, every couple that gets divorced started off with lots of things in common. That's usually why they got married, and with their divorce they prove that commonality isn't nearly enough to create a great relationship. Second, if you take this—finding someone who has things in common with you—to an extreme, you end up marrying another *you*. Boring. It's Real Love that makes a great relationship, not shared interests.

Long-distance Relationships

Can long-distance relationships work? Sure, for a while, but don't start dating someone who lives far from you unless one or both of you are willing to move.

People Who Have Children

When you date someone who has children, remember that you're dating the children's mother or father, not the children. If you try to ingratiate yourself too soon with the children, you'll introduce confusion into your relationship with the parent, and you'll make it harder for the children if your relationship with the parent doesn't work out.

Similarly, if you have children, don't push them on to your date too soon. It's too big a burden to carry early on.

Dating People at Work

Certainly it's possible to find a loving relationship at work, but remember that if the relationship doesn't work out, you'll have to interact with that person every day. Weigh the potential costs before you embark on this course.

Date as Many People as You Can

Date as often as possible. The more often you date, the faster you'll find the person you want to have an exclusive relationship with. Don't sit back and wait for people to call you. Reach out and make connections.

END OF THE DATE

So you've had a pretty nice date. Now both of you are standing by your car, or at the door of your apartment, saying goodbye. It often gets uncomfortable at this point. Does he/she really like me? Will there be another date? How do I express my feelings?

When in doubt, tell the truth. If you enjoyed the date, say so. Don't play coy little games with your partner. Those games waste time, and hurt people in the long run. In the next section, we'll explore some of the ways you can express your feelings about the date.

As you're expressing your enjoyment, you might gently touch or hold your partner's hand. That alone is an affectionate, intimate act, and you don't need to do more than that after a first date.

Hugging and Kissing

On a first date, you're still in the early stages of gathering information. Don't confuse your relationship with acts of intimacy that are greater than the actual depth of your relationship. Kissing and hugging are intimate behaviors. Don't use them until your relationship is farther along. An exception might be a brief "door-step" hug at the end of a date.

We'll talk about sex in dating in the next chapter.

SECOND DATES AND BEYOND: NO MORE WONDERING

We waste so much time and emotional energy wondering:

- Will he call again?

- Does she really like me?

- What's the next step in our relationship?

- Does he feel as close to me as I feel to him?

There's a lot we can do to eliminate all that needless confusion and worry.

Moving on to the Next Level

If you want the relationship to continue after the first date, don't sit around waiting. Women are famous for being coy at this point—they don't want to appear to be too eager. Ridiculous. If you want more from this relationship—both men and women—put more into it. At the end of the first date, say, "I really enjoyed being with you. I'd like to see you again."

Then wait to see if the other person says anything. If he or she says something affirming, like, "Yes, I'd like that," don't just leave it there. Go for it. Say, "I'll call you tomorrow (or Wednesday, or Friday), if that's all right. Or would you rather call me?" Or you could set up a second date right there.

If she agrees to your calling her, you darned well better call when you promised you would. Don't delay. The longer you wait, the more inconsiderate you're being, and the more she hears that you don't care about her. Breaking a promise once is a mistake; twice is a pattern.

If your partner says he/she would rather call you, that's often a way to tell you to get lost, but some people really are hard to contact, so they tend to do the calling. In any case, if someone elects to call you, wait a week to see if that happens. If not, call and see if there really is an interest on their part. Sometimes it helps to say, "Hey, I just want to see if you're interested in seeing me again. If you're not, my feelings will not be hurt."

Saying "No" to a Request for a Repeat Date

What if someone asks you for a second date, but you don't want to see him or her again? Do not play games. Don't make up stuff about being busy. Don't rationalize that just saying *no* will hurt somebody's feelings. It's far more unkind to create the impression that you want to be with that person when you really don't. The eventual breakup just gets messier the more you prolong it.

When you want to refuse a second—or later—date, say *no* directly and gracefully:

- "No, but thanks for asking."
- "No, I wouldn't, but it was flattering of you to ask."
- "I've enjoyed being with you tonight, but I'd rather just leave it at that. No insult to you. I just have my own idiosyncrasies about what I'm looking for."

If you reach out and touch his/her hand while you're saying *no*, they'll be more likely to feel your compassion, and feel less rejected.

After Three or More Dates

If you're being honest about yourself, and *if* you're looking for a serious, committed relationship—rather than just having a good time—you should know after three or four dates whether this is someone you want to have a long-term relationship with. After that much honest association, you should either be leaving the relationship, or you should be saying things like:

- "I'm enjoying the time I spend with you. A lot."

- "I really enjoying doing things with you."

- "I'm feeling relaxed and comfortable around you."

If your partner is not saying similar things, don't wonder what's going on. *Ask* him or her if she's feeling some of the same comfort, acceptance, and enjoyment that you are. You could say:

- "I've dated a lot of guys (or girls), but this relationship with you has been different from the others. I feel more accepted and comfortable around you than I usually do at this point in a relationship. I do *not* need you to feel the same (you'd better mean it when you say something like this), but I would like to know how you feel about our relationship. Would you be willing to talk about that?"

- "I'm really enjoying this relationship. How do you feel about it? And I'd like to know what you really think, not what you think I want to hear."

What you really want is someone who expresses those feelings without your prompting, but some people do need a little help in the beginning. Don't be afraid to learn that your partner doesn't like you. Remember from Chapter Four that you don't want to avoid rejection; you actually want to get to rejection faster, so you can move on with your life.

Displays of Affection

If you're developing a real affection for your partner, don't hide it. Express it with words, as described above, and use every other means at your disposal.

- Holding hands. This can be an intensely intimate demonstration of affection.

- E-mail. Just send little notes about what you're doing and thinking from time to time.

- A single flower. Doesn't have to cost anything. Pick it off the roadside.

- Notes in the mail.

Hugging and Kissing

As we discussed above, hugging and kissing can be quite intimate. Don't kiss your date until you're pretty serious about your relationship.

As you kiss your date, he or she will give you signs about whether your action is acceptable. If you see hesitation, stop what you're doing and say something:

- "Maybe I'm moving too fast. If so, tell me. I don't want to do anything you're not comfortable with."

- "I thought I saw some doubt in your face. Did I misunderstand that?"

We'll talk about sex in the next chapter.

ℬ *Chapter Seven* ℭ

The Mine Field

Sex in Dating

Everywhere we look, we see references to sex—books, movies, magazines, calendars, newspapers, television, radio, billboards, and the jokes and stories we tell one another. We actually look up to men and women who are known to be sexually attractive and sexually active, and we believe that if we're sexually appealing ourselves, we'll feel worthwhile and happy. Those of us who are not having an active sexual relationship are often portrayed as defective somehow.

In the United States, one-third of girls have had sex by age fifteen (compared with 5% in 1970), while 45% of boys have had sex by age fifteen (20% in 1972). 21% of nine graders have already had four or more sexual partners. One quarter of all adolescents contract a sexually transmitted disease before they graduate from high school.

The sheer prevalence of sexual activity among us dictates that we discuss the effect that sex is having on dating and on our relationships.

SEX AS A FORM OF IMITATION LOVE

We have established that in the absence of sufficient Real Love—
a condition that applies to the vast majority of us—we *will* try
to fill our emptiness with whatever forms of Imitation Love are
available to us. Sex can be an abundant supply of Imitation Love,
in all its forms: praise, power, pleasure, and safety.

When someone finds us sexually attractive, we feel an
enormous sense of worth (praise). Being seen as sexually
attractive, in fact, is perhaps the highest compliment in our
society, while being unattractive virtually makes one a leper.
As we discussed in Chapter Two, we can also use our sexual
desirability to get other people to do what we want, from
which we get a sense of power. The pleasure provided by sex is
obvious.

The combination of praise, power, pleasure, and safety
we feel from sex is so powerful that a great number of us are
obsessed with it. We see proof of this in so many ways:

- The most common use of the Internet for men is the
  search for pornography.

- Most commercials in magazines and on television attempt
  to sell their products with sex. By this product—drink
  this beer, buy this truck—and you will attract into your
  life a women as beautiful as the one in our commercial.
  Give your partner this gift, and she will have sex with
  you.

- As you listen to radio talk shows and to popular music,
  or watch television and movies, the references to sex are
  everywhere. An alien coming to earth and watching our
  entertainment would think that sex is all we think about.

- Most couples experience more tension about sex than
  about anything else.

> Sex can be a powerful form of Imitation Love. When we recognize that, we can avoid being seduced and distracted by it.

Trading Imitation Love with Sex

Most of us don't want to miss out on the bounty of Imitation Love derived from sex, so we respond by spending enormous amounts of time, energy, and money to look good—make-up, hair, clothes, plastic surgery, exercise. We then trade sex and other forms of Imitation Love to get all the Imitation Love we can get in return. We see this illustrated in the following story of Melanie and Blake.

When Melanie met Blake, she used all the tools available to her—clothing, make-up, hair, the way she spoke, the way she moved her body—to be physically appealing to him. Women often complain that men regard them only as sexual objects, but most women—to varying degrees, and more when they're younger—actually *work* at being sexual objects in order to get what they want. They trade sex—or at least the excitement they provide by being sexually appealing—for the praise, power, pleasure, and safety they want from the men in their lives.

We'll use Melanie and Blake's relationship to illustrate how men and women commonly use sex to trade Imitation Love, recognizing that the specifics vary from couple to couple. Throughout the chapter, I will generalize about how men and women get Imitation Love from sex. These generalizations are accurate most of the time, although there are relationships where the stereotypes do not hold. If your relationship doesn't fit the generalization—if, for example, she is more sexually aggressive than he is—simply switch in your mind the gender being described and continue to learn the intended principle.

Neither Melanie nor Blake had had much experience with Real Love, so when they met, they naturally tried to get as much Imitation Love from one another as possible, usually by offering it to the other in exchange for what they wanted. Sex was one way they could trade Imitation Love. In Chapter One, I talked about *dollars* as an arbitrary unit of measure for Imitation Love, and I'll use that unit again here.

Early in their relationship, Melanie felt about five dollars of praise from Blake—in the form of acceptance and actual compliments—because of her sexual desirability. Blake also felt complimented by Melanie's willingness to have sex with him, although the sense of praise he received was less than Melanie felt from him (two dollars for him, five dollars for her) .

Blake was quite accommodating about Melanie's wishes— where they went together, what they did—in great part because he noticed that when he did what she wanted, she was more sexually receptive toward him. Although she rarely manipulated him intentionally, Melanie felt important and in control when he did what she wanted. From sex she got five dollars of power. When Blake succeeded in getting sex from Melanie, that also gave *him* a feeling of power—two dollars.

They both found sex physically pleasurable, although Blake's enjoyment was greater than Melanie's (seven dollars versus two). Their mutual promise of sexual fidelity gave them both a feeling of safety, although Melanie felt less certain of Blake's faithfulness than he did of hers (two dollars of safety for Melanie, three for Blake).

This exchange of Imitation Love with sex can be summarized in the following table:

Type of Imitation Love	Dollars Received in the Relationship by	
	Blake	Melanie
Praise	2	5
Power	2	5
Pleasure	7	2
Safety	<u>3</u>	<u>2</u>
Total Imitation Love	14	14

Although Melanie and Blake experienced the various forms of Imitation Love differently when they had sex, the overall exchange was sufficiently rewarding and fair that they both enjoyed it very much.

It's easier now to understand why many people say that men give romance to get sex, and women give sex to find romance. What's happening is that through sex women offer physical pleasure—along with some praise and power—to get a return of praise and power for themselves. This trading is rarely conscious, but it's nonetheless a serious affair, with meticulous accounting, and both parties are quite aware when there is an imbalance in the exchange.

The Imbalance of Trade

After years of marriage, Blake and Melanie talked to me about how dissatisfied they had become with the sexual part of their relationship. He complained that they never had sex, and she complained that he was always pushing her to have sex, a scenario common in many relationships. I described to them why they had once enjoyed sex—because of the abundant and relatively equal exchange of Imitation Love detailed in the above diagram—and suggested that the balance of trade had simply become unacceptable to Melanie. The balance sheet now looked like this:

Type of Imitation Love	Dollars Received in the Relationship by	
	Blake	Melanie
Praise	1	1
Power	1	1
Pleasure	5	1
Safety	1	1
Total Imitation Love	8	4

Neither of them got much in the way of praise or power from sex any longer, for two reasons: First, the effect of Imitation Love had worn off, as it always does. The initial excitement that came from being praised for being sexually attractive, for example, had virtually disappeared. Second, as the effect of Imitation Love faded, neither partner was willing to give as much Imitation Love to the other, which further whittled away at the temporary satisfaction of the Imitation Love in their lives.

Although the overall enjoyment of sex had diminished for both of them, Blake was getting "twice" the Imitation love from sex that Melanie was, mostly because sex still gave him considerable physical pleasure. Because sex was still rewarding for him, he was willing to push for it, while Melanie didn't see it as something that gave her a sufficient return on her investment. Why should she be willing to participate in a trade that was so obviously unfair?

All couples who are now experiencing less sexual enjoyment than they once did are feeling the fading effects of Imitation Love, as well as an imbalance of trade. Most men initially offer praise, power, and safety in exchange for the physical pleasure women give them, and when men no longer "pay" sufficiently, women withhold the physical pleasure of sex. With most men, however—as with nearly all women—sex is much more than a physical experience. They really do need a feeling of warmth and connection, and they get little of that in most areas of their lives. At work, for example, they feel constant competition and criticism, but during sex they often feel a bit of the intimate warmth they need so badly.

For more about sex as a form of Imitation Love, see the book, *Real Love—The Truth About Finding Unconditional Love and Fulfilling Relationships* (Go to http://www.gregbaer.com/book/book.asp).

Sex Not Always a Form of Imitation Love

Although I have spoken negatively here about sex, I emphasize that sex is a form of Imitation Love only when it is used as a substitute for Real Love. Regrettably, because 90+ percent of us don't have sufficient Real Love, sex is used as a form of Imitation Love most of the time.

In an unconditionally loving relationship, sex is healthy, nourishing, fun. With Real Love sex becomes an *expression* of love, rather than a substitute for it.

SEX AS A DISTRACTION FROM REAL LOVE

As we discussed in Chapter Two, in the absence of Real Love all forms of Imitation Love are very appealing, and if we can get enough of it, we can briefly experience the illusion of happiness. We believe, however, that our happiness is real, and therein lies the destructive effect of Imitation Love—that it feels so good that we become obsessed with acquiring it, instead of taking the steps to find Real Love.

Imagine that you're starving to death in the middle of the desert, and in your wanderings you come across a truck filled with candy. What would you do? Eat, of course, until you were satisfied. Your satisfaction—the combination of taste, smell, and a full belly—seems so very real, doesn't it? But if you stay there by the truck, eating nothing but candy, you will die, because many of the nutrients essential to life are not found in the candy.

Similarly, the rewards of Imitation Love seem so very real, but as we pursue them, we starve to death, despite the rewards of taste, smell, and a full belly. The rewards of sex are so intense that we believe we have found true happiness, but without sufficient Real Love, it's all a fraud, distracting us from the pursuit of the Real Love we must have.

SAVING SEX FOR MARRIAGE

Precisely because sex feels so good, I strongly recommend that you do not have sex before you get married. I am not making a moral judgment here, only speaking from my experience with thousands of people. If you have sex early in a relationship, you'll have no idea what foundation your relationship has. You'll be so distracted by the taste of the candy that you literally will not be able to know whether your relationship is based on Real Love or Imitation.

Allow me to quote from *Real Love—The Truth About Finding Unconditional Love and Fulfilling Relationships*:

Imagine that you and I start work at a company on the same day, and we've never known each other before. As we become friends, I begin to give you a hundred dollars every time I see you in the hall. Of course, it wouldn't take long before you'd start creating opportunities to meet me in the hall, but both of us would inevitably begin to wonder – as you smiled at me each time – whether you were interested in *me*, for who I am, or in my money. Similarly, if you experience the pleasures of sex with someone early in a relationship — before you really know that person, before you've shared the truth about yourself, and before you've made an exclusive commitment to one another — you can't help becoming hopelessly confused. You lose your sense of what's true and what's real. You cannot know whether you care about your partner's happiness or whether you simply enjoy the way he or she pleases you sexually.

We can see these principles applied in real life as we observe my interaction with Jeff, a single man who had dated extensively.

Jeff: 	I'm really enjoying my relationship with Brittany, but I'm also aware that I've been using Imitation Love for so long, I could be kidding myself here. Maybe what I'm feeling isn't Real Love. How can I tell the difference?

Me: 	Are you sleeping with her?

Jeff: 	Yes.

Me: 	Quit.

Jeff: 	I don't understand.

Me: 	You get so much excitement—so much Imitation Love—from sex that you just can't be sure what your relationship is based on. Sex is *distracting* you, confusing you.

Jeff quit having sex with Brittany, and two weeks later he called to say that without the sex, their relationship just didn't have much to support it. "I'm beginning to see now," Jeff said, "what you've been telling me all along. I don't feel enough Real Love yet that I can have a genuinely loving relationship with *anyone*. I need to work on myself before I start dating, because right now the Imitation Love is just too seductive."

I recommend that people not have sex until they're married simply because sex is too distracting and confusing.

> Because sex can be enormously distracting and confusing as a form of Imitation Love, it's wise to avoid sex before marriage.

We've Proven That Sex Just Doesn't Work

Most people somehow recognize intuitively the truth of my recommendation to save sex for marriage. 73% of 12-14-year-olds who had sex said they wished they had waited. In a survey of adults of all ages, more than 90% wished they'd had sex later in their lives, and later in their relationships.

One of my daughters spoke to me one day about her observations of sex.

Daughter: Dad, at school it seems like everybody is having sex. The girls dress like whores, and the guys love it. They're all over them. The girls who are willing to have sex are the most popular, and sometimes I envy them. I want to dress and act like them, so I'll be as popular as they are.

Me: Are those girls happier than you? Really happy? Do they feel loved, and are they loving toward others?

Daughter: Come to think of it, no, they're not. Most of them are pretty unhappy and unkind.

Me: How long do their relationships last.

Daughter: (now laughing) I'm getting the point. They move from one guy to another. All they talk about is guys— the one they just left, the one they want, how they're manipulating the one they have.

Sex simply will not produce Real Love and rewarding relationships. We ourselves have proven that beyond all doubt.

If you're still experiencing the initial rush of sex, and believe that it will bring you happiness, I would certainly never try to stop you. Each of us has to learn in his or her own way that Imitation Love will never produce genuine happiness. I can tell you that if sex is your goal, it would be much cheaper—financially and emotionally—to simply hire a prostitute.

Saving Sex as Something Special for Your Spouse

We've established two great reasons to save sex until marriage:

- It's confusing and distracting
- We have proven by experience that sex before marriage doesn't lead to happiness

Now let's discuss a third reason:

- We can save sex as a unique expression of love for our spouse

Imagine that I've worked all morning to make for you the perfect dessert. Twelve layers of phyllo leaves I've made from scratch, dates from Saudi Arabia, honey from my back yard, crushed pecans. This might be the best thing you'll ever taste. On the way to your house, however, I pass a number of friends, and when they smell the dessert, they ask for a taste. I admonish each of them to take just a "little taste" around the edge, which they do. When I reach your front door, there is still a small piece left, but of course it has numerous tooth marks all around it. Some of the people who took a taste had been eating other things, so here and there you see bits of ketchup and mustard, and a coffee stain. How would you feel about your "gift?"

Now imagine that again I bake you the perfect dessert, but this time I refuse all the many requests I receive to have just a "little taste." Knowing that I had saved this treat just for you, do you not feel more loved than if I had shared my gift with everyone? Do you not feel more special and cared for?

And so it is when we save sex for our eventual spouse, and remain faithful after marriage. When we save certain behaviors—

sex, living together, shared finances—for one person, we are able to express our love with that person even more deeply than we can with others. It's well worth the saving.

Personal Experiences of People Who Have Made the Decision To Save Sex for Marriage

I'd like to share with you the personal experiences—shared with me by e-mail and phone—of people who have made the decision to save sex for marriage. Their experiences have been duplicated with positive results all around the world.

Kevin

"All my life, I have used women. I have stared at them, fantasized about them, and had sex with them. Recently I went on a date with a woman, and everything "clicked." I was in the process of fantasizing about her big time. I was planning when we were going to have sex and how we'd have sex, and then I started to remember some of the stuff I'd been reading in the *Real Love* book.

"I was horrified to realize that here she was telling me the story of her recent divorce, and sharing the pain in her life, but all I could think about was having sex with her. I couldn't believe how selfish I was being, and that I've been that way my whole adult life. Right there I made a decision that I wouldn't use a woman sexually again. I hate what it does to our relationship, and I hate how I feel after using her.

"Since then I've been spending a lot of time talking with friends on the phone, and meeting them in person, to talk about who I really am. And I'm participating weekly in a group of guys who are discussing the principles in the *Real Love* book. It's make a huge difference. Now when I date, I can focus on who she really is, not just what I want from her. I'm becoming confident now that I can find a relationship based on Real Love, instead of just sex. I'm grateful for the change."

Denyce

Denyce was physically beautiful and often used that characteristic to attract men. But she discovered the men she attracted only wanted to use her to gratify their own need for Imitation Love. She was quite unhappy with the many relationships she'd had and asked me for help.

Me: If you want unconditionally loving relationships, you'll have to stop using sex to attract men. I've watched how you behave around men. You're sexually seductive. Look at how you're dressed right now, for example. As long as you keep doing this, you'll keep attracting men who will use you.

Denyce: But if I quit dressing like this, and quit attracting men sexually, what would I have left?

Me: You'd have what you have right now with me. I don't want *anything* from you—sexually or otherwise— and I think you sense that.

Denyce: You're right, it *is* different with you, but you're happily married. How could I ever find this with a man who's single and looking for sex?

Me: Keep this simple. How do you feel with me right now?

Denyce: Safe, accepted, loved.

Me: *That* is what you need most in your life. Lots of it. At this point, you probably can't find that from a man, because you're tempted to attract him with sex, and he'll accept your offer. You need to have relationships with lots of women and maybe with old, ugly men like myself who aren't a potential source of sex for you. When you get enough of that, you'll feel healthy

and whole enough that you won't need to use sex to
attract men. You'll just tell the truth about yourself
and will find an unconditionally loving partner. *Until*
you get enough of that, *don't date* and don't look for
love from men.

Denyce followed this advice, and eventually she discovered
that without her offering sex, she was attracting an entirely
different—much better—class of men.

Sarah

Sarah had been widely sexually promiscuous. With her, the
question wasn't who she'd slept with, but who she *hadn't* slept
with. And she was miserable, proving again that no amount of
Imitation Love can ever make us happy.

I told her about how she could find Real Love in her life,
and at first she didn't take it seriously. Eventually, however, she
began to tell the truth about herself to some friends, and she
began to experience the healing effects of Real Love. She also
talked to me every other day or so.

One night, I received a call from Sarah. She said that her date
was in the other room, and she was beginning to feel pressured
to have sex. A big part of her wanted to comply and experience
the brief rush of praise, power, and pleasure that come from sex.
"But this time," she said, "I remembered how great it feels to be
loved unconditionally—by you and by my friends. So I decided
I'd rather call you, and feel the love you always give me, instead
of having sex with this guy."

Getting the Strength to Save Sex Until Marriage

We use sex as a form of Imitation Love only because we don't
have enough Real Love. The solution to giving up sex now
becomes obvious: We just need to get more Real Love, using the
process described in Chapter Four.

Simple will power and commitment are often not enough to keep us from using sex. Researchers at Columbia and Yale studied 12,000 adolescents who had pledged to remain virgins until marriage. 88% of them had premarital sex anyway. When we feel loved, however, we simply lose our *need* for Imitation Love.

Expressing Your Desire to Save Sex for Marriage

Once you conclude that saving sex for marriage is a wise decision, some people will undoubtedly think your being prudish, or holier-than-thou, or just plain stupid. It's helpful to practice ahead of time how you'll express your views on this subject to a date.

If he touches you in an sexual way, you might say, "I'd like to talk for a minute about your touching me. In no way am I criticizing you, just exploring what it means." If you say this with absolutely no irritation, with a desire simply to share something about yourself, you will have his full attention. Then you continue, "When you touch me like that, I wonder what your goal is. Are you trying to demonstrate a concern for *my* happiness, or are you looking to get a good feeling for yourself?"

If he then argues with you, pushing you to be sexual, you have your answer about what kind of person this man is. If he really listens and learns something, you might want to keep this one a little longer.

You might also add that you're not squeamish about sex itself. You simply want to save it for the most important person in your life. You could say, "I'm very interested in having sex with my husband, but not until then. I'd just like to see where our relationship goes without the distraction and confusion of sex. I'm certainly not afraid of sex. Eventually, when I get married, I'll be all over my husband sexually."

If you have sex to prove to your partner that you love him or her, you're doomed. That proving will never stop, and having sex certainly won't do it.

Expressing your position on sex before marriage is much more than words. You also express yourself with your behavior. If you say you want to save sex for marriage, but then your behavior is sexual, you're confused, and you'll confuse your partner. If you're serious about expressing your desire to save sex for marriage, you might consider the following guidelines.

- Be careful how much physical touching you do. Holding hands is pretty safe, but many other behaviors communicate a very sexual message: rubbing your body up against his or hers, sitting on his lap, giving a body massage.

- Anything but the most casual kissing. Intimate kissing is very provocative.

- Stay out of his or her bedroom. You have no good reason to be there.

- Never drink on a date. Alcohol depresses your higher—more sensible—brain functions and removes your inhibitions.

- Don't make your conversations sexual—in person or on the phone. You really don't need to start those fires.

But What about the Test Drive?

Many people have said to me, "But if I don't have sex with my partner until we're married, how will I know whether we're sexually compatible? Don't we need a test drive to be sure?"

Ridiculous. Can you imagine what it would be like to have sex with a partner whose primary concern was *your* happiness. Is there any way in the world that you wouldn't end up having great sex with someone like that?

After counseling with couples all across the country, I can tell you that sexual incompatibility is primarily caused by a lack of Real Love in both partners. Real Love simply makes for great sex. You do not need a "test drive" to prove that.

After you're married, your sexual experience could be enhanced by a knowledge of some things, and those are discussed in Chapter Eight of *Real Love in Marriage—The Truth About Finding Genuine Happiness in Marriage*.

If—after all this counsel to the contrary—you're still determined to have sex before marriage, at least be wise about it. Never have sex with someone unless you've had a direct, honest conversation about sex with that person—while you both have your clothes on, and without touching one another. You need to talk about birth control, the prevention of sexually-transmitted diseases (STDs), and any history of STDs.

INFIDELITY

Approximately 25-30% of wives and 45-50% of husbands have had extra-marital affairs. That's in *marriages*, so imagine the incidence of infidelity in couples who haven't made a commitment to be faithful to one another. Because few things affect the health and survivability of a relationship more profoundly than an affair, we need to talk about the causes of infidelity and how to respond to it.

The Causes of Infidelity

Since infidelity causes so much damage to relationships, why do people take the risk of being unfaithful? It's always about Real Love. In the beginning of a relationship, the exchange of Imitation Love is relatively equal and abundant, so both parties experience enough satisfaction that they believe they're genuinely happy. After a few weeks or months, however, both partners notice that the effect of Imitation Love wears off. They feel empty, alone, and afraid again.

Now what can they do? Usually they demand more Imitation Love from their partner, with more intensive use of Getting and Protecting Behaviors. But that never works for long, so eventually they go elsewhere for their supply of praise, power, pleasure, and safety. Having an affair simply provides a quick fix of Imitation Love—a fresh supply.

Responding to Infidelity

If your partner has an affair, remember that it's not about you. It's just his or her attempt to fill his emptiness. When you really understand that, your anger will go away. But the question now remains, should you stay in the relationship?

I can't answer that question for you. I *can* tell you that once you understand that the affair was just a product of insufficient Real Love—and the accompanying emptiness and fear—you can make a much more rational decision. You'll see that there are only two productive choices:

• Realizing that your partner is lacking in Real Love, you could make a commitment to find more Real Love from others, which you can then take back to your partner. If you consistently love your partner unconditionally, the chances are high that you will be able to fill his or her emptiness, after which he or she will have no reason to be unfaithful to you. You would make this choice only if you are *strongly* committed to this relationship.

OR

• You could decide that your partner's infidelity is a strong sign that he or she simply isn't capable of participating in an unconditionally loving relationship. It might be wiser— certainly more efficient—if you break away from your partner, get more Real Love for yourself, and start over with better tools. As I mentioned in Chapter Five, it's easier to climb a mountain without a hundred-pound pack than with one.

For more about dealing with infidelity, see Chapter Eight of *Real Love in Marriage—The Truth About Finding Genuine Happiness in Marriage.*

Varieties of Infidelity

Most of us agree that being faithful to a partner means that we won't have sex with other people. Without having sex, however, you can still be unfaithful to your partner in many ways. Some of these include:

- Looking at other women (or men) with any sexual interest whatever. We're often quick to claim that we're just looking innocently, but if you look at other women with any more interest than you would look at a tree, your interest is sexual.

- Touching other men or women in a way that you wouldn't touch your brother or sister.

- Flirting.

Before you claim to be innocently flirting with someone, you need to ask yourself these questions.

- Do you share with your partner the conversations you have with this "friend?" You don't need to share with your partner every word you say to other people, but at least would you be *willing* to share if asked?

- Do you say negative things about your partner to this person?

- Would you feel comfortable if your partner were watching and listening to a videotape of your conversation?

- Do you touch each other differently when you're alone than when you're with other people?

- Do you ever wonder what it would be like to have sex with this person?

Prevention of Infidelity

Although it's important to understand the causes and varieties of infidelity, it's more important to understand how we can keep it from ever happening. If you follow these steps, you won't find your attention wandering from your partner:

- Talk frequently to your partner about your other friends, and what you do with them. Don't keep secrets.

- Tell your partner the truth about your mistakes and Getting and Protecting Behaviors. That will create the opportunities for you to feel genuinely accepted by him or her, and make it unlikely that your sexual attention would wander to others.

- Tell the truth about yourself to other people, and as you fill up with Real Love, you'll lose any need to find the artificial excitement of sexual intimacy outside your present relationship.

- Avoid placing yourself in situations where you'll be physically alone with people toward whom you feel sexual attraction.

ℬ *Chapter Eight* ℜ

The "M" Word

Making the Commitment to Marriage

Julia came to my office to talk about the relationship with her fiance, Brian. They had been dating for almost a year, but recently Julia had been learning about Real Love.

Julia: We have a wedding scheduled in one month, but now I don't know what to do. It's obvious he's never been loved unconditionally, and I'm beginning to see that I haven't, either. I'm in the process of learning how to love him unconditionally, but so far he hasn't shown any interest in learning about Real Love. What do you think I should do?

Me: I can't tell you whether you should or should not marry someone, but I can ask you some questions that might help you make your decision.

Julia: That would be great.

Me: If gold were available, would you settle for lead?

Julia: What do you mean?

Me: Real Love is the gold standard in relationships. It's the greatest thing in the universe. Are you willing to settle for a relationship based on anything other than Real Love? Are you willing to settle for lead?

Julia: No, the more I learn about Real Love, the more I know that I want a relationship like that.

Me: Has he shown any interest in being completely honest with you, and in learning how to love you unconditionally?

Julia: Well, we do have fun together, and we have lots in common.

Me: Meaningless. Every couple that gets divorced had fun in the beginning, and they had lots in common. But without Real Love, all that means nothing.

Julia: But I am learning how to love *him* unconditionally. Isn't that enough?

Me: That's up to you. If you marry him before you are certain about whether he can learn to love you unconditionally, you're taking an enormous risk with your happiness. You're playing Russian roulette, just as surely as though you were doing it with real bullets.

Before you even think about marrying someone, you need to assess whether Real Love is the foundation of your relationship. Marriage alone should never be the goal.

WHEN ARE YOU READY TO MARRY?

When we talk about marriage, we tend to focus on finding the right partner. Before you consider *whom* to marry, however, it's critical that you first ask yourself if *you* are prepared to be an unconditionally loving spouse. Sophia demonstrates the importance of who we are in the process of finding a partner as she talks with me about her dating and marriage experiences.

Sophia has been married three times and has recently had a series of brief relationships with men. "I have the worst luck," she says. "In the beginning, every guy I marry—and most of the guys I've dated—looks like he'll be perfect, but then he turns out to be a rat, like all the rest. I don't get it. Where are the good men in the world? Are there any?"

I couldn't help but chuckle. "Sophia," I said, "have you considered the possibility that you keep catching rats because *you* are rat bait?"

That wasn't what she wanted to hear, but it was exactly what she needed to understand. Sophia had always felt unloved and empty. With her behavior and words, she was virtually a walking billboard that said, "I'm empty and desperate, and I'll do whatever it takes to eliminate those feelings. If you'll give me the praise, power, and security I need, I'll give you lots of attention, praise, and sex." She didn't *realize* she was broadcasting that message, and the men she attracted couldn't have put it into words, but they nonetheless *sensed* her needs, as well as the rewards they'd get from the relationship if they temporarily gave her what she wanted. As a trader in Imitation Love, she naturally attracted men who were also traders in that commodity—and then she was surprised and disappointed at what she got.

Sophia began to understand and find Real Love, however, and then she wasn't satisfied with trading Imitation Love any longer. As she became a different person—interested in receiving and sharing Real Love—she naturally began to attract an entirely different kind of partner. She called me one day to talk about that. "I'm amazed," she said. "There really are some decent guys out there. Where were they before?"

"They were always there," I assured her, "but they weren't attracted to the bait you were offering. Everything around you begins to change when *you* are different yourself."

If you lack sufficient Real Love—and are therefore empty and afraid—you will not be able to function in a healthy relationship, nor will you attract a healthy partner. You must honestly examine yourself for signs of emptiness and fear as you look for a partner. For example, you might ask yourself:

- Do I feel lonely?

- Do I worry about not having enough dates?

- Do I worry about what my partner will think of me?

- Am I looking for somebody to make me happy?

- Am I crushed when I break up with someone I've been dating?

- Do I worry about how I look and what I'll say when I'm on a date?

If you exhibit these signs, your emptiness and fear will cause you to seek Imitation Love and significantly distract you from the kind of relationship you really need.

Before you're capable of finding a healthy intimate or exclusive relationship, you must eliminate your own emptiness and fear—not completely, but to a large extent—with the Real Love you need. You can get that love from *anyone* who has it— friends, family, and so on. In Chapter Four, we talked about how to tell the truth about yourself and find these loving people.

In Chapters Four and Six, we talked about how you can know whether you're ready to date. The criteria for marriage are similar. Don't even consider getting married:

- When you feel empty and afraid. In that condition, you

will manipulate your partner for Imitation Love, and you'll protect yourself, making a loving relationship impossible. How can you tell if you're empty and afraid? When we've been empty and afraid for a lifetime, we often fail to notice those conditions—they seem quite normal. It is sometimes easier to identify the symptoms of emptiness and fear: Getting and Protecting Behaviors. If you are often angry, or withdrawn, or act like a victim, or lie, you *are* empty and afraid.

- Until your partner knows everything about you. If you have secrets, you'll forever wonder if he or she would love you if the secret were known.

- Until you are certain that your partner is capable of being honest about his or her mistakes, flaws, fears, and Getting and Protecting Behaviors. Can he or she easily admit being wrong? Is your partner committed to learning how to love you unconditionally. Perfection isn't required here, but real evidence of intent is. We'll talk more about choosing a partner in a later section.

> Don't even think about getting married until you have enough Real Love that you are not desperate for the love of a spouse.

You also need to have direct, serious discussions with your partner about many things before you marry:

- Money. Who will manage what? What kind of accountability will you require of one another?

- How you will handle conflicts that will inevitably arise. You can learn a lot about that in Chapter Four of *Real Love in Marriage—The Truth About Finding Genuine Happiness in Marriage.*

- Sex. Will you both feel free to initiate sex? When one person doesn't want sex, and the other does, how will you handle that?

- Children. Do you want them? How many? What if you disagree about this? Who will be responsible for what parts of the children's care? How will you deal with misbehavior?

- Residence. Should your careers require one of you to move to another city, will the other person gladly move, or would you turn down a promotion so you could both stay in the same city?

- Family—parents and other relatives. Can both of you accept all the members of both families? Or will there be friction associated with some of those relationships?

- How will household responsibilities be divided?

- Religion. How will different religions play out in your marriage? How will the children be raised?

- Smoking and drinking? Will these be part of your lives? If so, will it be allowed in the house? With the children?

- Career. Will both of you work for a living? One of you? Do you anticipate getting additional education?

Reading *Real Love—The Truth About Finding Unconditional Love and Fulfilling Relationships*

One additional criterion has been suggested to me by many people who have succeeded in the process of finding an unconditionally loving partner. They have written and called to tell me this:

Don't even think about marrying somebody—or for that matter, dating them more than twice—unless he or she will read *Real Love—The Truth About Finding Unconditional Love and Fulfilling Relationships* with you, and discuss it. (Go to http://www.gregbaer.com/book/book.asp). If a partner expresses no interest in those principles, why would you want to marry someone like that?

Getting married is probably the biggest decision most of us will ever make. Don't be in a rush. Never settle for less than Real Love.

> If you read *Real Love—The Truth About Finding Unconditional Love and Fulfilling Relationships* with your partner, you'll usually learn in a hurry whether he or she is genuinely interested in an unconditionally loving relationship.

"I Love You"

These are powerful words to communicate to a partner, and unless you see that person as a potential spouse, you would be wise to keep these words to yourself.

WHY DO PEOPLE AVOID COMMITMENT?

Why are so many people reluctant to make the commitment to get married? Let's suppose that you've expressed your love to a man, and he just won't make a commitment to you. What's the problem?

When a man has had little experience with Real Love—although I choose a man here, most women have the same problem—he has a hard time imagining anything but Imitation Love. When you say, "I love you," what he really hears you say is this: "I love how I feel when I'm around you, and I need you to keep making me feel good. Now that I've put myself out on a limb and told you my intimate feelings, I need you to do the same. I need you to love me, too. I expect it, in fact."

In response to that perceived message, his thoughts run amok, including a combination of the following:

- "What do you want from me? The people in my life have always wanted something in exchange for whatever they gave, and I have no reason to suppose that you would be any different."

- "Sure, but what will I have to do so you'll *keep* loving me?"

- "Do I really want to take on the responsibility of doing everything it will take so you'll keep loving me?"

- "I wonder how long this will last?"

- "So what? Lots of people have told me that, and I didn't end up happier because of it."

- "When are you going to hurt me like everyone else who's claimed to love me?"

- "I suppose now I'll have to tell you I love *you*, or you'll be hurt and angry."

- "But I don't know if I'm *capable* of returning your love in the way you want."

We're afraid of making a commitment only because we are overwhelmed by the following fears:

- Somehow we sense that the thrills of Imitation Love we enjoy in the beginning of a relationship will not last. We've seen the fleeting effects of Imitation Love all our lives, and even though we're pretty excited about the abundant flow when we're in love, we have doubts that it will continue.

- We're afraid that we just don't have what it takes to love our partners in the ways they need. Falling in love is fun, but we realize that it can't be a one-way street. We can't just *receive* love from our partners. We also have a responsibility to love them, and we're not sure we can do that.

Is it any wonder, then, that many people are reluctant to make a lifelong commitment to keep struggling with all the doubts, fears, and obligations outlined in the two lists above? With all those fears, it's a miracle that anyone ever overcomes them long enough to make a commitment.

HOW DO YOU HANDLE A PARTNER WHO WON'T COMMIT?

If you're in a relationship where you desire a commitment, but your partner is resistant, what can you do? As we suggested in Chapter Four, with every relationship or situation, we have three choices:

- Live with it and like it
- Live with it and hate it
- Leave it

I've lost track of how many people have called me and revealed that they have made the second choice. They persist in a relationship—sometimes for years—with a partner who will not make a commitment, all the while resenting their partner and trying to change him or her. The second choice *never* leads to happiness, so don't make it. It's the other two choices we need to consider.

Live with It and Like it

If your partner is resisting commitment, one of two situations exists:

- You're not loving him or her unconditionally. For the reasons we discussed in the previous section, our partners are afraid of making a commitment to any relationship based on Imitation love. You're loving your partner as well as you know how, but it simply isn't Real Love. If you haven't received sufficient Real Love yourself—which is the case with 90+% of us—there's no way you can give that kind of love to a partner. You reveal in many ways that your love isn't unconditional: disappointment when he or she doesn't make a commitment, for example.

- You are loving your partner unconditionally, but he or she is so overwhelmed by fear that he just can't feel the Real Love you offer. Some of us are so occupied with Getting and Protecting Behaviors, that we turn everything we get into Imitation Love.

Be very slow indeed to assume that your relationship falls into the second category. Very few of us are loving our partners unconditionally, and because of that my first recommendation to those of you whose partners are slow to commit is to do what it takes to get more Real Love in your lives. Tell the truth about yourself every day to people you judge might be capable of loving you, and as you feel their unconditional acceptance, share that with your partner. As your partner feels the healing power of Real Love, it's likely that he or she will change his attitude toward making a commitment with you. People are naturally attracted to Real love. You must be very careful here, however, not to love your partner better *so that* he or she will make a commitment. In that case, you'd just be manipulating him or her, and your partner will feel that.

Leave It

So now let's suppose that you are loving your partner unconditionally, but he or she still will not make the commitment you would like for marriage. You have only two choices that make any sense. Either you happily live in a relationship without commitment, or you leave the relationship. If commitment matters to you, but your partner continues to be reluctant—despite your freely offering Real Love to him or her—he is telling you that he's not ready for a loving relationship. Accept that decision and move on.

HOW CAN YOU KNOW YOU'VE FOUND THE PERFECT MAN/WOMAN?

We all want the perfect partner, and that's just fine as long as we understand a workable definition for *perfect*. In some ways, it would be nice if we could find a partner who always loved us, never got in our way, knew what we wanted, and gave us what we needed without our ever having to ask for it. But such partners don't exist, and until we become flawless ourselves, it seems hypocritical and arrogant to think that we *deserve* such a partner.

What we *can* have is a partner who will walk by our side and *learn* to build a relationship with us founded on Real Love. That is a perfect partner.

Most people begin their marriages believing they've found The One for them—otherwise they wouldn't have married that person—but then they discover that things are not what they had believed. In great part, their disillusionment was guaranteed when they began looking for entirely the wrong qualities in a potential spouse.

The greatest aim of life is to have the genuine happiness that can only come from receiving and giving Real Love. Obviously, you want as a spouse someone who can contribute to that kind of happiness in your life, but you're not likely to find such a person when you begin with an incorrect notion about the characteristics that your partner should have, a notion demonstrated here by Laurie.

Laurie: You can probably tell I'm pretty excited. I've been dating this guy for a while, and I really feel good when I'm with him. I think he's getting close to asking me to marry him, but I don't want to regret this decision later. How can I know for sure if this is the guy I want to marry?

Me: Tell me about him.

Laurie: There's a lot to tell. He's good looking, and smart, and has a great job. He takes me out all the time, and we enjoy so many of the same things—the same movies, sports, all kinds of things.

Me: So it sounds like he has the qualities that rank 12, 14, 18, 20, and 24 in importance.

Laurie: I don't understand.

Me: Imagine that you go with me to a buy a new car, and I find one that has great looking chrome, a beautiful paint job, nice leather upholstery, and a really fine stereo system. I tell you that it has everything I've been looking for, but you point out that it doesn't have an engine, or tires, or a transmission. Would you think I was wise to pay full price for that car?

Laurie: Of course not.

Me: Why?

Laurie: If the car doesn't have the important stuff, it doesn't matter what else it has. It won't run.

Me: Exactly, and if a prospective husband doesn't have what matters most, it doesn't matter what other great qualities he has. As you talk about your boyfriend, you describe qualities that number 12, 14, and so on in importance, but you haven't mentioned the ones that really matter. Without them, you're not going to like how that car runs.

The Most Important Qualities

Let me list—in descending order of importance—the qualities in a partner that most determine success in marriage.

1. A willingness to tell the truth and learn how to be unconditionally loving.
2. A willingness to tell the truth and learn how to be unconditionally loving.
3. A willingness to tell the truth and learn how to be unconditionally loving.
4-10. A willingness to tell the truth and learn how to be unconditionally loving.
11-100. Everything else.

If you marry a partner who lacks the ability to be honest, and who doesn't have a burning desire to be unconditionally loving, you will sorely regret choosing that person on the basis of a great body, entertaining sense of humor, perfect teeth, a promising career, and every hobby in the world in common with you. I have seen many people marry based on an astonishing abundance of qualities 11-100, but their marriages have failed for a lack of qualities 1-10.

> What you really want most in a partner is a willingness to tell the truth, and a desire to learn how to be unconditionally loving. Everything else is a distant second.

It's one thing to understand that the ability to be truthful and a desire to learn to be unconditionally loving are important qualities. It can be quite another thing to *identify* those qualities in a partner, especially since most of us have had little experience with them. You'll be able to better identify these important abilities in a partner as you ask yourself the following questions about him or her:

- When you tell the truth about yourself—especially about your flaws, mistakes, and fears—does he become uncomfortable and change the subject? Is he critical? Does he try to fix you?

- Can she easily admit that she's wrong—about her mistakes, about being selfish when she's angry, and so on? Or when she's wrong, does she dismiss it like it didn't happen, or make excuses, or argue with you and insist that she's right?

- When you're talking about yourself, does he listen intently—focusing entirely on what you're saying, asking questions about *you*, and clearly demonstrating that what you're saying is important—or does he seem to be waiting for the next opportunity to get in a word of his own?

- Does she tend to find fault with other people, putting them down for their mistakes and flaws?

- When you correct him, does he gratefully accept your observation, or does he defend himself and become irritated?

- Does he tend to boast about his accomplishments, and does he often portray himself as being in a superior position to someone else?

- If you inconvenience her or fail to do what she wants, does she become disappointed and irritated?

- Is he grateful for what you do and who you are, or does he tend to notice what you *don't* do for him and complain about the qualities you don't have?

- Does he/she criticise what you are wearing, who you talk to, what you read or study, your political opinions, your friends, how you act?

- Does he/she demand to know your every move throughout the day?

- Does your partner's *behavior* match his or her *words*? It's behavior that tells the truth.

- Is he/she lazy? Does he tend to avoid anything that would involve intense or steady effort?

- Does he or she drink? Smoke? Use drugs?

These are important questions. If your partner doesn't intently listen to you now, while he's courting you and trying to win your favor, how do you think it will be when he's not trying so hard? If she can't easily admit being wrong, she'll soon be blaming you for everything that goes wrong in her life. If she finds fault with everyone around her, *you'll* be next, and when you're married, you'll be the primary focus of her criticism and blaming. If he enjoys being in a superior position to other people, after you get married you can be certain that he'll put himself in a position superior to you, too. If he gets annoyed with you for inconveniencing him now, it will get much worse when he thinks he owns you.

It's not enough to have a partner who's entertaining and fun to be with. You need a partner who can love you. Don't look for a partner who is perfect, who has none of the negative qualities I listed above. There aren't many of those out there. These are just guidelines. As you consider marrying someone, you need simply to ask yourself, If my partner remains as he presently is—with all the negative qualities—could I live with him or her for the rest of my life, *assuming that I learn to be more accepting and loving*? That last phrase is important, because if we're not accepting, we'll never find a partner with whom we could live happily. As we become more accepting and loving, we can live with a lot of characteristics that might be bothersome to us now.

Once you've found someone who is truthful and actively involved in the process of learning how to love other people unconditionally—including you—you've hit the jackpot. You may also want that partner to have some of the other qualities that add spark to a marriage—qualities 11-100, as we discussed earlier—but don't get too hung up on those, because they don't determine the success of a marriage. Any two people who are truthful and loving can make a loving relationship. Whether you want to *marry* that particular person is a question only you can answer.

THE EXPECTATIONS OF MARRIAGE—NATURAL BUT DEADLY

Although marriage can be the most rewarding experience in life, it can also be the greatest source of disappointment and frustration. You can begin to see some of the reasons for this as you watch Marcia talk to me about her husband, Shawn.

I just don't get it," she says. "When we first got married, you couldn't pry us apart. We did everything together. Now he hardly wants to do anything with me. He just watches television by himself, and when I suggest that we go out and do something, he's always too tired. This is not how I thought marriage would turn out."

"You seem irritated."

"Of course I am. Who wouldn't be?"

"*I* don't spend much time with you—certainly less than Shawn does—and I never go out with you. Why aren't you irritated with *me*?"

"Oh, come on. That's different. You're not my husband."

Marcia was more angry at Shawn than at me because she had much greater *expectations* of him. We get disappointed and angry only when people don't behave as we *expect*. If you expect nothing at all from someone, his or her behavior simply can't be a source of disappointment to you.

The expectations we have of our spouses are very high— after all, we married them *because* we thought they would make us happy—and such expectations inevitably result in disappointment, anger, and conflict. When most of us got married, both we and our partners had failed to receive sufficient Real Love, a condition that began long before we met one another. This lack of Real Love is intolerably painful, and to eliminate our emptiness and fear, we seek Imitation Love from everyone around us. When we meet someone who gives us Imitation Love in sufficient quantity, we experience a temporary satisfaction we confuse with genuine happiness. We fall in love with people who give us enough of that temporary "happiness," and we may even marry them in the hope that they will continue to make us feel that way all our lives.

When two people get married, they exchange promises that boil down to this: "I will always love you more than I love anyone else." That's what each partner *says*, but each person *hears* the other say much more:

> I promise to make you happy—always. I will heal your past wounds and satisfy your present needs and expectations— even when you don't express them. I will lift you up when you're discouraged. I will accept and love you no matter what mistakes you make. I give to you all that I have or ever will have. And I will never leave you.

Neither partner is consciously aware of making these many promises, but each partner still hears them and desperately insists they be fulfilled. When we feel empty and unloved, we understandably expect the people around us—especially those who claim to love us—to give us what we want and make us feel better. In the case of a spouse, where we have received a solemn promise of love, we feel especially justified in having those expectations.

In most marriages, however, neither partner has the Real Love his or her partner needs, so they both struggle constantly with the impossible task of trying to make one another happy.

Because our principal motivation for getting married is our powerful expectation that our partner will love us and make us happy, our disappointment and anger are then colossal when we don't achieve those goals.

When our partner doesn't fulfill our expectations, we respond by insisting even more urgently, which begins a pattern of mutual manipulation or outright resistance but certainly doesn't produce the Real Love we want. Although our attitude is understandable, we often use our marriage vows as a whip to force our spouses to give us what we want, but this approach can only be frustrating and cause great unhappiness. Even in marriage, expectations are usually selfish, because the Law of Choice still applies.

THE REAL PURPOSE OF MARRIAGE

So what *is* marriage? *Marriage is a commitment* we make to stay with our partner while we *learn* to unconditionally love *him* or *her*. It's an agreement to stay in a relationship for a lifetime, even when our partner isn't loving. It's also a commitment to limit the sharing of some things (living together, sex, financial resources, and so on) to one partner.

That may not be a romantic definition of marriage, but it is clear and useful, which I'll demonstrate as I respond to a question that invariably arises when people hear that definition. For example, many people wonder, "Since almost all partners are not unconditionally loving, why in the world would I *want* to get married in the first place and make a lifetime commitment to share my body, my financial resources, and so on with only one person? It doesn't sound like marriage is such a great idea."

> Marriage is not a means of obligating our partner to do what we want. Marriage is a commitment we make to stay with our partner while we *learn* to unconditionally love *him* or *her*.

If we view marriage as an opportunity to squeeze all the Imitation Love we can get out of another person, marriage usually *doesn't* turn out very well, since the effects of Imitation Love always wear off, and the trading of it becomes unfair. But when we see marriage as an opportunity to learn to love another person unconditionally, making such a commitment to one person is quite rewarding. Sex, praise, financial resources, and everything else we have become tools with which we express affection for our partner. When we reserve some of those tools exclusively for one partner, we're able to communicate a more profound level of loving with that person.

You can learn a great deal more about marriage by reading *Real Love in Marriage—The Truth About Finding Genuine Happiness in Marriage.*

℘ *Chapter Nine* ℭ

Do I Leave, or Do I Stay?

What to Do with Difficult Relationships

Our relationships start with such high hopes, don't they? We find someone who gives us feelings of satisfaction and excitement greater than we've known with anyone else, and then we eagerly anticipate that those feelings will continue forever.

But so often it all begins to fall apart. Our expectations are not met, the ensuing disappointment and frustration are overwhelming, and finally the relationship ends, shattering the dreams we once had. It can be such a painful process. We can eliminate most of the pain associated with ending a relationship, however, if we follow three general guidelines:

- Decide *whether* each relationship can be what you want, rather than *trying to make it* what you want.
- End relationships sooner.
- End relationships lovingly.

As I discuss relationships throughout this chapter, I am referring only to non-married relationships. Divorce is discussed in the last chapters of *Real Love—The Truth About Finding*

Unconditional Love and Fulfilling Relationships ([http://www.](http://www.gregbaer.com/book/book.asp)
[gregbaer.com/book/book.asp](http://www.gregbaer.com/book/book.asp)) and *Real Love in Marriage—The
Truth About Finding Genuine Happiness in Marriage.*

DECIDE *WHETHER* EACH RELATIONSHIP CAN BE WHAT YOU WANT, RATHER THAN *TRYING* TO MAKE IT WHAT YOU WANT

Rachel came to talk to me about the relationship with her boyfriend,
James. They had been dating for a year. In the beginning, they
had a great time together, but now they were arguing almost
constantly—about how to spend their time together, about their
families, about sex, and lots of little things.

Rachel: I really want to keep this relationship together. What
can I do?

Me: Why would you *want* to keep it together?

Rachel: I love him, and he loves me.

Me: I do believe that you're doing your best to love him,
but that doesn't mean you *do* love him.

Rachel: How can you say that?

Me: The only kind of love that counts is Real Love—
unconditional love. Everything else isn't love at all—
it's just neediness and Imitation Love. Think about
what you've told me here this evening. The two of
you fight all the time, and you think it's about a variety
of subjects, but it's really all about one thing—You're
both angry that the other person doesn't listen to what
you want. Neither of you really believes that your
partner cares about you. That's a *huge* problem.

I really do believe that part of you wants James to be

happy, but primarily you're interested in getting what *you* want. Your anger proves that. You're not primarily interest in *his* happiness, which is the definition of Real Love. That's no accusation of either of you, just a description of how things are. Neither of you ever received enough Real Love—from childhood on—to be capable of a loving relationship.

Your relationship was pretty much doomed from the moment you said *hello.* It started off great— the Imitation Love was really flowing between you—but when the Imitation Love wore off, the disappointment was enormous. You began to use Getting and Protecting Behaviors with one another— that's what your arguments are all about—and it only got progressively worse from there.

Rachel: So what are you suggesting?

Me: The relationship you have now is not based on Real Love. Would you be satisfied to be in a relationship like this for the rest of your life?

Rachel: No.

Me: Then you need to revise your goals. When we first started talking, you said you wanted to keep this relationship together. That's not a productive goal if this relationship can only produce Imitation Love, disappointment, and unhappiness. Your goal shouldn't be to preserve this particular relationship, but instead to find and develop a relationship that is based on Real Love. That *might* happen with James, but it might not.

I then explained to Rachel what I say to almost every couple whose relationship has become difficult.

- If you're married to your partner, you've made a lifelong commitment to learn how to love your partner. You need to take the steps to find Real Love for yourself—Chapter Four—and then take that love back to your spouse. In most cases, if you will consistently love your spouse unconditionally—and tell the truth about yourself—he or she will lose the need to use the Getting and Protecting Behaviors that have been damaging your relationship, and your relationship will change dramatically.

- If you're not married to your partner, you have to decide whether you want to stay in a relationship that has already proven to be unloving, or do you want to learn more about Real Love and start over in a relationship that is based on Real Love from the beginning? Do you want to climb the mountain of life with or without a hundred-pound pack on your back—as explained in Chapter Five.

> Never try to force a relationship to succeed. Just observe whether it could become what you want, and if not, let it go.

If you're not married, and you decide that you really do want a relationship based on Real Love, there are three ways to go:

- Stay with your present partner while you find the Real Love that may transform your relationship.

- Leave your present partner so you can find the Real Love that will change your next relationship.

- Stay with your present partner while you find the Real Love that may transform your relationship. If that approach fails, leave your partner so you can find the Real Love that will change your next relationship.

Starting Over—With Your Present Partner

A relationship without sufficient Real Love *cannot* bring you the kind of happiness you want. If you want to change such a relationship, the only person you can control is yourself. If you want to stay with your present partner, you must take the steps to find Real Love—described in Chapter Four of *Real Love in Dating*, and in *Real Love—The Truth About Finding Unconditional Love and Fulfilling Relationships*—and bring that love back to your partner.

If your partner then *receives* the love you offer, he or she will be lifted out of the pool—Chapter Three. He'll no longer be drowning, and won't have the need to use the Getting and Protecting Behaviors that have been destroying your relationship.

I caution you, however, that staying with your present partner while you learn to find the Real Love in your life can be very difficult, for a number of reasons:

- With your present partner, there are so many wounds and disappointments that poison any effort to feel and behave differently. Many people simply cannot let those old wounds go.

- With your present partner, you have enormous expectations. As you begin the process of finding Real Love, you'll almost certainly find those expectations— and the ensuing disappointments—very distracting.

- If you're having difficulty with your partner, both of you are clearly demonstrating that you don't have the Real Love required for a healthy relationship. Developing a great relationship is hard enough—why work on one that is seriously flawed, when you could start over with better tools and a partner already more willing and able to participate in a relationship based on Real Love? Why try to renovate a house that's falling apart, when it would be much faster and cheaper to build a new one?

If you're willing to live with those imposing obstacles, it is possible to resurrect some relationships that have become unworkable. If you find the Real Love you need, and share it with your partner, you can often make a big difference. Most of us, however, are impatient as we try to share our love with our partners, as demonstrated here by Rachel, several weeks after my initial interaction with her. She decided to stay with James, read the *Real Love* book, and see if that made a difference in their relationship. As we began our conversation, she was quite irritated.

Rachel: I did what you said, but it didn't make any difference at all.

Me: What did you do?

Rachel: I read the *Real Love* book, but when I tried to explain it to James, he didn't want anything to do with it.

Me: You seem annoyed.

Rachel: Sure. I put a lot of effort into this, but it was a waste of time.

Me: You read the *Real Love* book how long ago?

Rachel: I finished it a couple of weeks ago.

Me: (chuckling) And how many times have you told the truth about yourself—your mistakes, flaws, and Getting and Protecting Behaviors—with people who are capable of really loving you unconditionally?

Rachel: (pausing) I haven't really had a chance to do that yet.

Me: So let me get this straight. You've understood the principles of Real Love for only a couple of weeks, and you've actually *experienced* none of the Real Love that would be required for you to interact with James without using your Getting and Protecting Behaviors. And then you thought you'd make a difference in James's life?

Rachel: I hadn't thought of all that.

Me: You thought you could change your approach to James a little bit, and he would immediately reward you. You wanted something in return for your effort, which is the essence of conditional love. How you feel and behave with James is a result of a *lifetime* of not feeling loved unconditionally. You're not going to change that with a little effort. It's going to take a lot more effort than you've made so far.

Shortly we'll talk about what Rachel did.

Starting Over—Without Your Present Partner

Another approach to a difficult relationship is to recognize that from the beginning of your relationship the two of you simply didn't have what was required—Real Love—to make it work. Rather than trying to renovate the house that's falling apart, you could leave your partner and take the steps to find Real Love elsewhere. You'd have the advantage of doing this without the expectations, disappointments, and wounds of the past relationship. Once you have enough Real Love, you will then attract healthier partners, and will find it much easier to participate in an unconditionally loving relationship.

Real Love isn't the icing on the cake in a relationship; it *is* the cake. Real Love isn't something else to do in life; it *is* life. No effort you make to get more Real Love will ever be too much.

Many people are very reluctant to let go of their present relationship, even though it is severely flawed. Why are we so resistant to giving up on a relationship that doesn't work? Most flawed relationships "survive" only because both partners are motivated by fear to stay together. We often stay together out of a fear of:

- Being alone. Sure, we may fight with our partner, but some companionship—even when it's often difficult and manipulative—can seem better than none at all.

- Letting go of our dreams. When we form a relationship, we have huge expectations of what it will be like. We have dreams of a level of happiness we've not known before, and abandoning those dreams is an awful feeling.

- Admitting we're wrong. When a relationship fails, *somebody* has to be at fault, and we do not want to be blamed by others for anything.

- Not being able to find something better. Our partner may have lots of faults, but what if we can't find anyone better? After all, we started this relationship certain that we had found the best. What if there simply isn't anything better?

- The unknown. This relationship may be difficult, but what if everything else is even worse?

- Inconvenience. We naturally like to do whatever is easiest, and breaking up is not convenient.

- Hurting our partner. We do not want to be responsible for the pain our partner feels if we leave.

- The condemnation of other people. Nothing spurs gossip like a juicy break-up, and we don't want to be the subject of everyone else's advice, criticism, and condescension.

- Not keeping a commitment. If in our present relationship, we made a commitment to stay with our partner, breaking up is a painfully obvious failure to do what we said.

I cannot tell you whether you should stay with your present partner. I can tell you, however—as I suggested earlier—that building a house from the ground up, with the best tools available, is usually much easier than renovating—with flawed tools—a house that is falling apart. For that reason, I recommend that you stay with a partner in a seriously flawed relationship only if:

- You're married.

OR

- You have an overwhelming belief that this relationship is the only one that could make you happy.

> If a relationship is difficult, the answer always involves you finding more Real Love in your life, with or without your present partner.

Staying with Your Present Partner, and Then When That Doesn't Work, Leaving and Starting over

After I talked to Rachel above, she made the decision to really put her best effort into finding the Real Love she needed. She read the *Real Love* book again, and she also read *The Wise Man—The Truth About Sharing Real Love*. She shared the principles of those books with her friends, and they began to meet weekly to practice being honest and loving one another. She was quite a different person when she talked to me months later.

Rachel: I've never been this happy.

Me: You even look different.

Rachel: Until recently, I had never known what it feels like to really be honest about myself, and to feel the unconditional acceptance of others.

Me: Nice, isn't it?

Rachel: The best. I have to admit, though, that I'm not seeing
           a lot of difference in my relationship with James. I
           can be loving with other people pretty well, but when
           James starts getting angry, I have a much harder time
           not reacting badly.

Me: You just have greater expectations of James. You
           expect him to love you, so when he doesn't, you feel
           disappointed and irritated.

Rachel: So far, no matter what I do, he still gets irritated at
           me pretty easily. In fact, my relationship with him is
           the hardest part of my life. I'm beginning to wonder
           if I'd be better off starting over.

As you find more Real Love in your own life, you will be
happier, whether you stay with your present partner or not. If
you choose to stay with your partner, and after a time—only you
can know how long that time is—you determine that staying in
your present relationship has an overall negative effect on your
happiness, you might be wiser to leave your partner and start
over.

If you are lacking in Real Love, do *not* leave your partner
and immediately replace him or her with another. If you do that,
you'll end up right back where you were in the old relationship,
because *you* will be the same person. Be very slow to begin
another relationship. Allow many months to pass, perhaps a year.
In that time, devote yourself to finding and sharing Real Love
with others. As you feel more loved, as you feel more loving, and
as you become more whole and happy, you will then be capable
of participating in an unconditionally loving relationship. You
will also discover that you attract an entirely different kind of
partner into your life.

Eventually, Rachel did leave James—in a later section, we'll talk about the best way to do that—and continued finding the Real Love she needed from friends. Eight months after the above conversation, she came to see me again.

Rachel: I have a new relationship.

Me: Tell me about it.

Rachel: After I left James, I did what you suggested. I concentrated on feeling more loved, and on learning how to love others. As I felt more complete, my emptiness and fear went away more and more. I became much happier, and then I discovered something I wouldn't have anticipated: People wanted to be around me more. And the men who wanted to be with me were really different from the kind of men I used to find. I guess my old emptiness and fear were more obvious than I realized, because I used to attract men who used my emptiness. They could see that I was willing to trade Imitation Love with them, so they gave me what I wanted in exchange for getting what *they* wanted.

Me: And now?

Rachel: I still run into guys who are looking to trade Imitation Love, but I don't find that the least bit attractive anymore. So there's no chance of my starting a relationship with a guy like that. I started finding men interested in being honest, interested in me for who I really am. And now I'm dating one of them pretty often.

Me: How's that working out?

Rachel: I'm amazed at the difference. I really care about his happiness, and he cares about mine. We're honest with one another. We don't play games. We talk things out. We didn't start our relationship with sex. He's reading the *Real Love* book with me, and we're having a great time.

If you are in a troubled relationship—not a marriage—I usually recommend that you think seriously about whether your path to genuine happiness will be helped or hindered by staying with your present partner. If you conclude that your present relationship would be a difficult road to walk, you might consider leaving it. Then, after getting the Real Love you need, you'll do much better in a future relationship.

If you're not sure about leaving, I recommend that you do what Rachel did. Try to find Real Love and share that with your partner. If there's not a dramatic response to the love you offer, you can re-consider whether it would be wise to leave that relationship and start over.

How long should you try to revive the old relationship before giving up? We'll talk about that in a subsequent section.

It's Easier to Prevent a Difficult Relationship than to Fix One

In Chapter Six, we discussed the criteria to consider before you even begin dating. If you will heed those, and not date while you're empty and afraid, you won't even start those relationships that are doomed from the beginning, the ones that cause so much pain.

END RELATIONSHIPS SOONER

We discussed this subject in Chapters Four and Six. If your relationship is not unconditionally loving, and if it doesn't have a strong possibility of growing in that direction, you might consider letting it go. The sooner you do that, the faster you can move on to the kind of relationship you really want.

Ask yourself the following questions about your present partner:

- Is this the man/woman I want to spend a lifetime with? Do I want to grow old with this person—just like he or she is now?

- Is this the father or mother I would want for my children?

- Is it highly likely that I'll experience a lifetime of shared joy with this person?

If your answer to these questions is *no*, move on. If you're worried about hurting his or her feelings, remember that if you prolong your departure, more emotional energy will have been invested, and the break-up will only get more difficult.

> Don't hang on to relationships that are not clearly moving toward Real Love. Let them go, and let them go quickly.

Choose to pay less—in time and pain—for the lessons in your life. Get to "no" faster, as we discussed in Chapter Four.

END RELATIONSHIPS LOVINGLY

Once you've decided to leave your partner, what's the best way to do that? Never leave a relationship while you're angry, or while you're blaming your partner. If you think your partner is to blame, you'll repeat the same pattern in the next relationship, and you don't want to do that.

First, you need to recognize for yourself why the relationship ended. Your relationship started on the basis of an abundant exchange of Imitation Love. Neither of you had enough experience with Real Love to make a genuinely loving relationship possible. When the effects of Imitation Love wore off, you were left with great disappointment, after which the Getting and Protecting Behaviors steadily escalated. You were both drowning—Chapter Three—and it is simply impossible for two drowning people to help one another. When you understand all that, the anger and guilt wash away. How can you be angry at someone—your partner or yourself—for drowning?

Now you're in a position to tell your partner why you're leaving. There are many things you can say, among them:

- "I'm so sorry for the pain I have caused you in this relationship. I've been learning a lot lately about what Real Love is, and I realize that I haven't been nearly loving enough with you—or anyone else, for that matter. I need to be on my own while I learn more about Real Love. Staying in a relationship while I learn is just too distracting."

- "This is not about you. It's all about me learning to be more loving."

- "Please don't take this personally. I just don't know how to love you in the way you need, and that is not your fault."

- "I really did want to make this work with you, but I just wasn't able to. My fault."

- "Our relationship isn't what I'd hoped, and I take complete responsibility for that. Now I'm going to learn how to participate more lovingly in a relationship, and I need to be on my own to do that."

Notice that in all of the above expressions, you're not saying anything negative about your partner. Never make it about him or her.

> When you recognize that relationships don't work because of a lifelong lack of Real Love in the lives of both parties, you can let go of anger and guilt when a relationship ends.

"Let's Just Be Friends."

Sometimes, in an effort to soften the blow, you might say to a partner you're leaving, "Let's just be friends." Platonic friendship between two ex-partners is possible, but most of the time it's just too confusing for both parties. If you attempt to be friends immediately after your break-up, the old wounds and expectations won't just disappear, and you'll likely find yourself frustrated by the effects of those old feelings.

It's usually wiser to stop a relationship completely. As you become more loving, and when you've moved on to another relationship, you may be able to develop a friendship with an ex-partner.

Talking about Your Break-up

When you tell other people you've left a relationship, there is a strong tendency for them to believe that somebody had to be at fault. We love placing blame. In an effort to avoid being seen as the defective partner, you may feel an urge to point out the flaws of your partner. Do not give in to this temptation. Instead, tell the truth. You could say something like this:

> In order for a relationship to succeed, it has to be based on unconditional love. I've discovered that I'm simply not loving enough yet to be in a relationship. So now I'll be working on that.

Never blame your partner. If someone persists in asking what part your partner played in the break-up, you could say,

"You know, I've learned that the mistakes of other people are just none of my business."

The Destructive Power of Anger

In the process of ending a relationship—making the decision and every subsequent stage of living with it—anger is a common feeling. That's understandable—after all, look at the justifications we can provide for our irritation:

- You promised to love me, but you didn't.

- Now I'll be alone, and it's *your* fault.

- Now I have to go through the awful process of finding another partner.

- You've made me look like a fool.

- I've lost some of my friends because they've sided with you.

- And so on.

We get a real payoff from being angry: We feel less helpless, we can get people to side with us, we appear to be in a morally superior position, and we're distracted from the emptiness and fear that are always the real problems. The short-term rewards of anger are many, but it never produces genuine happiness. Never. Your blaming and anger will only hurt you, your ex-partner, and others. Anger is the biggest obstacle to making wise choices and being happy. It will poison you and everyone around you.

So what *should* you do if you become angry? Take the five steps for dealing with anger, as described in Chapter Nine of *Real Love—The Truth About Finding Unconditional Love and Fulfilling Relationships.* Certainly you can talk about your anger—you need to do that in order to feel loved unconditionally—but not to the person you're angry at *while* you're angry. Instead of blowing up at your ex-partner, talk to a friend about your anger, and describe the real cause—the lack of Real Love in your life, your expectations, and your selfishness—which will create an opportunity for you to feel accepted and loved. It's Real Love you want, and you can feel the healing power of that love when you get it from any source—not just from your ex-partner.

AFTER THE BREAK-UP

Many people obsess over a break-up for a long time. They blame their ex-partners for their misery, or they heap guilt upon themselves, or they do a combination of both activities. They ask, "How could he do this to me?" Or they say, "If only I had ___." We spend so much time grieving our losses in the past and worrying about what bad things might happen in the future—all a waste of time. How much better it is to have faith that if we just do the next right thing now, we'll be happy. And the right thing is so simple. If you'll keep telling the truth about yourself, you will create opportunities for people to accept and love you, and you *will* feel loved. Then you'll learn to love others, which results in the greatest happiness imaginable.

Think about your past relationships only in terms of what you can *learn* from them. How were *you* selfish? What Getting and Protecting Behaviors did you use with your partner? What can you do to increase the Real Love in your life, which will enable you to avoid making the same kinds of mistakes again? Remember that your partner's mistakes are not your concern. He or she was drowning and using the Getting and Protecting Behaviors that briefly kept his or her head above water. You have no right—nor the ability—to judge what he or she should have done differently. Let it go.

Afterword

To learn more about the basic principles of Real Love, read *Real Love—The Truth About Finding Unconditional Love and Fulfilling Relationships*, found at all major bookstores and at http://www.gregbaer.com/book/book.asp

For a workbook that multiplies the practical effect of the *Real Love* book, read *The Real Love Companion—Taking Steps Toward a Loving and Happy Life*, found at http://www.gregbaer.com/book/book.asp

To learn more about how to share Real Love with others, read *The Wise Man—The Truth About Sharing Real Love*, found at http://www.gregbaer.com/book/book.asp

To learn how the principles of Real Love apply in marriage, read *Real Love in Marriage—The Truth About Finding Genuine Happiness in Marriage*, found at http://www.gregbaer.com/book/book.asp

To learn how to use Real Love in parenting, read *Real Love in Parenting—A Simple and Powerfully Effective Way To Raise Happy and Responsible Children*, found at http://www.gregbaer.com/book/book.asp

For a set of three 60-minute CDs that describe the principles of Real Love in an abbreviated fashion, listen to *The Truth About Love and Lies*, found at http://www.gregbaer.com/tapes/tapes.asp

For the complete audio recording (eight hours of listening) of *Real Love—The Truth About Finding Unconditional Love and Fulfilling Relationships*, go to http://www.gregbaer.com/tapes/tapes.asp

For a video recording (150 minutes, two DVDs) of a presentation by Greg on the subject of Real Love—before a live audience—listen to *The Healing Power of Real Love*, found at http://www.gregbaer.com/tapes/tapes.asp

For more information of any kind, write to us a mike@gregbaer.com

Printed in the United States
21993LVS00004B/220-270